Contents

D1628646

Acknowledgements

The publishers are grateful for permission to reproduce copyright material. It has not always been possible to identify the sources of all the material used, and in such cases the publishers would welcome information from the copyright owners.

Illustrations by Chartwell Illustrators.

Design concept by Peter Ducker MSTD

Cover design by Dunne & Scully

The cassette/CDs which accompany this book were recorded at Studio AVP, London.

To the student

This book is for students preparing for University of Cambridge ESOL Examinations Key English Test (KET). It contains four complete tests based on the new test format from March 2004.

What is KET?

KET is an examination for speakers of other languages studying English. It tests Reading, Writing, Listening and Speaking. The KET examination is at Cambridge Level One (Council of Europe Level A2).

Paper 1	1 hour 10 minutes	**Reading and Writing**	9 parts	50% of total marks
Paper 2	approx 30 minutes	**Listening**	5 parts	25% of total marks
Paper 3	8–10 minutes	**Speaking**	2 parts	25% of total marks

How do I prepare for KET?

It is important to know what type of questions are in the KET examination. Doing the tests in this book will help you. Practise putting your answers on the sample answer sheets on pages 82–84 (you may photocopy these pages). This will help you to understand what you have to do in the real test.

Reading: Read some books in simple English from your library or local bookshop. Try to guess the words you don't know before you use a dictionary to check them. Also, use an English learner's dictionary when you study. If you live in a tourist area, there may be some signs or notices in English outside restaurants and shops or in railway stations and airports. Read these and try to understand them.

Writing: Write short letters or messages in English to a friend who is learning English with you or find an English-speaking pen-friend/e-friend to write to. Write about your daily life (your home, work or school and your family). If you go on holiday, write postcards in English and send them to your English-speaking friends.

Listening: Listen to the cassettes or CDs that come with English coursebooks so you can hear different people speaking English. Watch English-language programmes on television and listen to English on the radio if possible.

Speaking: Talk in English with friends who are studying with you. Ask each other questions about your daily lives, your future plans and about other towns, countries or places you have visited.

We hope this book helps you when you take the KET examination. Good luck!

Test 1

PAPER 1   READING AND WRITING (1 hour 10 minutes)

PART 1

QUESTIONS 1–5

Which notice (A–H) says this (1–5)?
For questions 1–5, mark the correct letter A–H on the answer sheet.

EXAMPLE	ANSWER
0 This is broken.	C

1   Children pay less than adults here.

2   Be careful because this will burn.

3   We don't want any money yet.

4   Things are cheaper here.

5   You must pay with cash.

A
> **SUMMER SALE**
> **LOW PRICES IN ALL**
> **DEPARTMENTS**

B
> FIRE DOOR
> KEEP CLOSED

C
> LIFT NOT WORKING

D
> TOY SHOP NOW OPEN

E
> BUY NOW
> PAY NEXT YEAR!

F
> Keep this nightdress
> away from fire!

G
> We do not take cheques
> or credit cards.

H
> Under 12s
> HALF PRICE

PART 2

QUESTIONS 6–10

Read the sentences (6–10) about going to the zoo.
Choose the best word (A, B or C) for each space.
For questions 6–10, mark A, B or C on the answer sheet.

EXAMPLE   **ANSWER**

0   On Sunday, Tim .... up early because he was going to the zoo.   **B**

   A   stood   **B**   woke   **C**   went

---

6   He put some biscuits and an apple in a bag for his ....

   A   meat   **B**   lunch   **C**   dish

7   He took a bus to the zoo and got off outside the .... entrance.

   A   high   **B**   important   **C**   main

8   He .... at the monkeys eating some bananas.

   A   enjoyed   **B**   watched   **C**   laughed

9   The lions were sleeping under a tree because it was very ....

   A   hot   **B**   tired   **C**   full

10   Tim .... some photos of the elephants.

   A   put   **B**   took   **C**   made

PART 3

QUESTIONS 11–15

Complete the five conversations.

For questions 11–15, mark A, B or C on the answer sheet.

EXAMPLE	How are you?	A I'm 18.	ANSWER
		B I'm Peter.	C
		C I'm fine.	

11   John's broken this plate.

    A   That's very good.

    B   Here you are.

    C   It doesn't matter.

12   Is this your watch?

    A   It's three o'clock.

    B   I think it's Dave's.

    C   I'm sorry I'm late.

13   Can I have a sandwich?

    A   Yes, of course.

    B   Yes, it is.

    C   Yes, that's right.

14   How many people were in the café?

    A   Not much.

    B   A few.

    C   A little.

15   We're from London.

    A   Not at all.

    B   Yes, please.

    C   How interesting.

QUESTIONS 16–20

Complete the conversation about a flat.

What does Ben say to Ann?

For questions 16–20, mark the correct letter A–H on the answer sheet.

EXAMPLE	ANSWER
Ann: 279616, Ann Beaton speaking.	
Ben: **0**	D

Ann:	Oh yes, in the Evening Post?	**A**	How many bedrooms does it have?
Ben:	**16**		
Ann:	£300 a month.	**B**	That's right. How much is it?
Ben:	**17**		
Ann:	Two, both of them with double beds.	**C**	OK. Can I come and see it?
Ben:	**18**	**D**	Hello, I'm phoning about your advertisement for a flat.
Ann:	Yes. It's quite small, but there are some nice plants in it.		
Ben:	**19**	**E**	Is there a bus stop near the flat?
Ann:	I'm afraid not, but you can park outside on the street.	**F**	Does it have a garden?
Ben:	**20**		
Ann:	Of course – is tomorrow all right? At about 10 a.m.?	**G**	How many beds are there?
Ben:	Yes, that'll be fine. So I'll see you tomorrow. Goodbye.	**H**	And is there a garage?

PART 4

QUESTIONS 21–27

Read the article about some birds.
Are sentences 21–27 'Right' (A) or 'Wrong' (B)?

If there is not enough information to answer 'Right' (A) or 'Wrong' (B),
choose 'Doesn't say' (C).

For questions 21–27, mark A, B or C on the answer sheet.

CANADA GEESE

Canada Geese are large blue and white birds. When autumn arrives, they have to fly south where the weather is warmer. The winters are so cold in Canada that the birds die if they stay there.

Last spring, Bill Lishman found sixteen young Canada Geese on his farm. They had lost their parents. Bill thought, 'These young birds won't know what to do in the autumn.'

Bill had a small plane and he decided to teach the birds to follow him. All through the summer, he went on short trips in his plane and the young geese flew after him.

When the cold weather arrived in autumn, Bill flew to Virginia in the United States, 600 miles south of his home in Canada. The geese followed him all the way. Bill left the geese in Virginia and he returned home.

This spring, Bill was waiting for the birds to come back. They didn't arrive, so Bill flew to Virginia to get them. He looked for them for two weeks but he couldn't find them.

When he arrived back home, Bill found the geese waiting for him. They had found their way home without him!

EXAMPLE	ANSWER
0 Winters in Canada are too cold for Canada Geese. **A** Right **B** Wrong **C** Doesn't say	**A**

21   Bill Lishman is a farmer.

   A Right   **B**   Wrong **C**   Doesn't say

22   Bill lives with his parents.

   A Right   **B**   Wrong **C**   Doesn't say

23   Bill carried the geese in his plane.

   A Right   **B**   Wrong **C**   Doesn't say

24   This was Bill's first visit to Virginia.

   A Right   **B**   Wrong **C**   Doesn't say

25   Bill wanted the geese to stay at his home for the winter.

   A Right   **B**   Wrong **C**   Doesn't say

26   Bill stayed in Virginia all winter.

   A Right   **B**   Wrong **C**   Doesn't say

27   The geese returned to Canada in the spring.

   A Right   **B**   Wrong **C**   Doesn't say

PART 5

QUESTIONS 28–35

Read the article about bicycles.

Choose the best word (A, B or C) for each space (28–35).

For questions 28–35, mark A, B or C on the answer sheet.

BICYCLES

The bicycle is ....**0**........ cheap and clean way to travel. The first bicycle ....**28**........ made about one hundred and fifty years ago.

At first, bicycles were expensive. Only rich people ....**29**........ buy one. These early bicycles looked very different from the ones we have today. Later, ...**30**........ bicycles became cheaper, many people ....**31**........ one. People started riding bicycles to work and in ....**32**........ free time.

Today, people use cars more than bicycles; cars are much ....**33**........ and you don't get wet when it rains! But some people ....**34**........ prefer to cycle to work. They say that ....**35**........ are too many cars in town centres and you can't find anywhere to park!

EXAMPLE			ANSWER
0 **A** some	**B** any	**C** a	C

28 **A** was	**B** is	**C** were	
29 **A** must	**B** could	**C** may	
30 **A** when	**B** if	**C** that	
31 **A** buy	**B** buys	**C** bought	
32 **A** their	**B** his	**C** its	
33 **A** fast	**B** faster	**C** fastest	
34 **A** yet	**B** still	**C** already	
35 **A** they	**B** there	**C** here	

PART 6

QUESTIONS 36–40

Read the descriptions (36–40) of some people in a family.

What is the word for each description?

The first letter is already there. There is one space for each other letter in the word.

For questions 36–40, write the words on the answer sheet.

EXAMPLE	ANSWER
0 If your child is a boy, he is this.	s o n

36 This is your mother's brother.

u n c l e

37 She is your father's mother.

g _ _ _ _ _ _ _ _ _

38 This is the person a man is married to.

w _ _ _

39 This is your father's sister.

a _ _ _

40 If your child is a girl, she is this.

d _ _ _ _ _ _ _

PART 7

QUESTIONS 41–50

Complete these letters.
Write ONE word for each space (41–50).
For questions 41–50, write your words on the answer sheet.

Dear Sir,

I (Example: __read__) your advertisement for English courses __41__ the newspaper. I would __42__ to have some more information. How __43__ does a course cost? Also, __44__ long is each course and when does the next course start?

Yours,

Maria Gonzalez

Dear Ms. Gonzalez,

Thank __45__ for your letter. Our next course starts in three weeks, __46__ Monday, 9 May. This is a 6-week course and it __47__ £150. If you prefer __48__ begin in June, we have __49__ 10-week course for £200. I hope __50__ is the information you want.

Yours,

David May

PART 8

QUESTIONS 51–55

Read the note from a student who wants a book from a library.
Fill in the information on the Reservation Form.
For questions 51–55, write the information on the answer sheet.

Rose Cottage
Northfleet
26 March

To: Weston University Library

My teacher, Robin Gibson, has told me to read *Understanding Science* before my exam on 17th April. I am on holiday in Northfleet at the moment but I'll return to my home at 22 King's Road, Weston on 9th April. I'd like to get the book the next day and keep it for one week. It's by S J Renshaw. Thank you.

Mary Jones

Weston University Library

Reservation Form

Name of book:	*Understanding Science*
Name of writer:	**51**
When do you want the book?	**52**
For how long?	**53**
Student's name:	**54**
Student's address:	**55**

PART 9

QUESTION 56

Your friend has asked you to go swimming tomorrow evening. You can't go.
Write a note to your friend.

Say:

– **why** you can't go
– **when** and **where** you can meet your friend on another day.

Write 25–35 words.
Write your note on the answer sheet.

PAPER 2   LISTENING (approximately 30 minutes including 8 minutes transfer time)

PART 1

QUESTIONS 1–5

You will hear five short conversations.

You will hear each conversation twice.

There is one question for each conversation.

For questions 1–5, put a tick ✓ under the right answer.

EXAMPLE

0   How many people were at the meeting?

3	13	30

A ☐   B ☐   C ✓

---

1   What will they eat for dinner this evening?

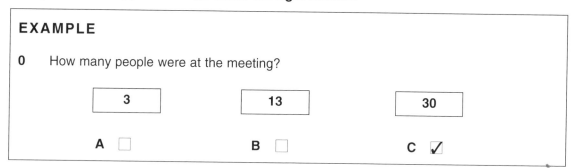

A ☐   B ☑   C ☐

2   What time is it?

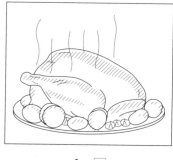 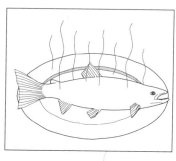 

A ☐   B ☐   C ☐

3 What's Michelle going to read?

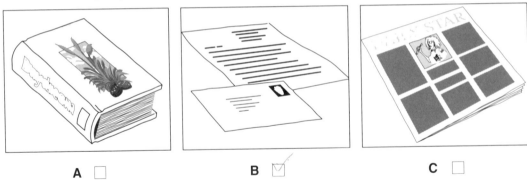

A ☐   B ☑   C ☐

4 How much did the tickets cost?

A ☐   B ☑   C ☐

5 Where is the chemist's?

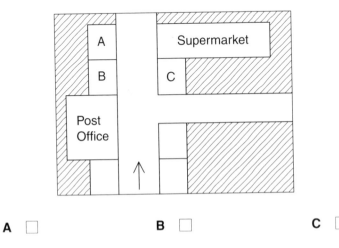

A ☐   B ☐   C ☑

PART 2

QUESTIONS 6–10

Listen to Kate telling Emma about her family.
Where is each person going today?

For questions 6–10, write a letter A–H next to each person.
You will hear the conversation twice.

EXAMPLE	ANSWER
0 Sam	B

PEOPLE

6	Kate's mother	E
7	Tanya	D
8	Len	A
9	Tom	C
10	Kate's father	G

PLACES

A   concert

B   dentist's

C   driving school

D   golf club

E   hairdresser's

F   shops

G   Spanish class

H   tennis club

PART 3

QUESTIONS 11–15

Listen to a woman talking to a policeman.
For questions 11–15, tick ☑ A, B or C.
You will hear the conversation twice.

EXAMPLE			ANSWER
0 Where did the woman lose her bag?	**A**	in town	☑
	B	on the bus	☐
	C	at home	☐

11 How much money was in the bag?	**A**	£20	☑
	B	£40	☐
	C	£50	☐
12 What else was in the bag?	**A**	credit card	☐
	B	driving licence	☐
	C	gloves	☑
13 The bag was	**A**	old.	☑
	B	expensive.	☐
	C	big.	☐
14 What time did the woman lose the bag?	**A**	9.30	☐
	B	10.00	☐
	C	10.30	☐
15 The policeman will telephone her in the	**A**	morning.	☑
	B	afternoon.	☐
	C	evening.	☐

PART 4

QUESTIONS 16–20

You will hear a man speaking on the telephone.
He wants to speak to Miss Dixon, but she is not there.

Listen and complete questions 16–20.
You will hear the conversation twice.

Message

TO:		Miss Dixon
FROM:	16	Mr HYDE
Meeting about:	17	new today
On:		Wednesday
Time:	18	11:30
In:	19	room 2
Please take:	20	bring a photograph

PART 5

QUESTIONS 21–25

You will hear a man talking about a day trip.

Listen and complete questions 21–25.

You will hear the information twice.

DAY TRIP

To:	Loch Ness
Breakfast at:	21 7:30
Meet in:	22 behind the hotel
Colour of lunch ticket:	23 pink
Get lunch ticket from:	24 restaurant
Bring:	25 a jacket

You now have 8 minutes to write your answers on the answer sheet.

PAPER 3   SPEAKING (8–10 minutes)

The Speaking test lasts 8–10 minutes. You will take the test with another
candidate. There are two examiners, but only one of them will talk to you. The
examiner will ask you questions and ask you to talk to the other candidate.

Part 1 (5–6 minutes)

The examiner will ask you and your partner some questions. These questions will
be about your daily life, past experiences and future plans. For example, you may
have to speak about your school, job, hobbies or home town.

Part 2 (3–4 minutes)

You and your partner will speak to each other. You will ask and answer
questions. The examiner will give you a card with some information on it. The
examiner will give your partner a card with some words on it. Your partner will use
the words on the card to ask you questions about the information you have. Then
you will change roles.

Test 2

PAPER 1 READING AND WRITING (1 hour 10 minutes)

PART 1

QUESTIONS 1–5

Which notice (A–H) says this (1–5)?
For questions 1–5, mark the correct letter A–H on the answer sheet.

EXAMPLE	ANSWER
0 We are only open in the morning.	G

1   Not all drivers can stop here.

A   **SWIMMING POOL ADULTS ONLY 6–8 p.m.**

2   Children cannot come here in the evening.

B   TELEPHONE for customers' use only

C   **DANGER!** No Traffic Lights Ahead

3   Drivers must be careful.

D   PARKING FOR POLICE CARS ONLY

E   LEEDS CASTLE FREE ADMISSION FOR CHILDREN

4   Not everyone can make a call from here.

F   Film matinee 2 p.m. £3.00

5   Only adults have to pay here.

G   Bookshop – Closed afternoons

H   **TELEPHONES ON SECOND FLOOR**

PART 2

QUESTIONS 6–10

Read the sentences (6–10) about a swimming pool.
Choose the best word (A, B or C) for each space.
For questions 6–10, mark A, B or C on the answer sheet.

EXAMPLE	ANSWER
0 A new swimming pool has just .... in the town centre.	**A**
A opened **B** built **C** become	

6   Everyone must .... a shower before they go in the water.

    A   do   **B**   make   **C**   take

7   There are special changing rooms for .... with young children.

    A   brothers   **B**   parents   **C**   cousins

8   Please .... to take a towel with you to the pool.

    A   know   **B**   understand   **C**   remember

9   If you are .... , you can get a drink in the snack bar upstairs.

    A   dirty   **B**   thirsty   **C**   wet

10   In the afternoons, there are swimming classes for children of all ....

    A   ages   **B**   lessons   **C**   pupils

PART 3
QUESTIONS 11–15

Complete the five conversations.
For questions 11–15, mark A, B or C on the answer sheet.

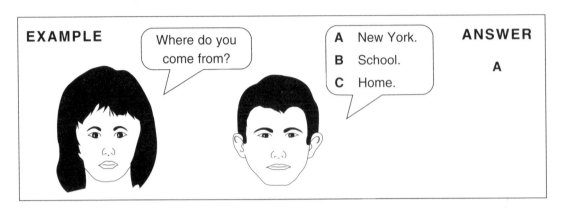

| EXAMPLE | Where do you come from? | A New York. B School. C Home. | ANSWER A |

11 John's going to London.

A Often?
B Yesterday?
C By train?

12 When do you study?

A At school.
B In the evenings.
C In the library.

13 Do you like my new shoes?

A Where did you buy them?
B How long are they?
C Would you like them?

14 Be careful.

A Thank you.
B I will.
C What a pity!

15 I hate basketball.

A You are, too.
B It can, too.
C I do, too.

QUESTIONS 16–20

Complete the conversation between two friends.
What does David say to Sarah?
For questions 16–20, mark the correct letter A–H on the answer sheet.

EXAMPLE	ANSWER
Sarah: Hello, David. How are you?	
David: **0**	**D**

Sarah:	I'm tired. I went to see a late film last night.	**A**	Perhaps I'll go next weekend.
David:	**16**		
Sarah:	That one with Brad Pitt, the American actor.	**B**	Are the tickets expensive there?
David:	**17**	**C**	Oh, what did you see?
Sarah:	I think so. You liked his last film, didn't you?	**D**	Fine thanks, and you?
David:	**18**	**E**	Do you think I'd like it?
Sarah:	The new one in the city centre.	**F**	Is the city centre far?
David:	**19**	**G**	Yes, it was really good. Which cinema did you go to?
Sarah:	Yes, £6, but it's much better than the old one.		
David:	**20**	**H**	You should go to bed early.
Sarah:	Well, I hope you like it.		

PART 4

QUESTIONS 21–27

Read the article about Esther and then answer the questions.
For questions 21–27, mark A, B or C on the answer sheet.

ESTHER'S STORY

When Esther left school at the age of sixteen, her aunt Flory gave her £500 for her birthday. Most of Esther's friends decided to go to college, but Esther used her aunt's money to start her own business. She bought fruit, sugar and some glass jars and began making her own jam. She sold the jam for £1 a jar to her friends and she soon doubled her aunt's £500.

At first, her parents didn't want Esther to spend her time making jam and they thought that she should study instead. They hoped that one day she would be a teacher or a doctor. But Esther didn't listen to them. She just kept on making jam. After a few months, she started selling it to the local market. Then she started making orange juice. She sold this to a school where one of her friends worked.

After two years, her business was very large and her parents were very pleased with her. She made all kinds of food which she sold to shops and supermarkets. She was so busy that she had to get some people to work for her.

EXAMPLE			ANSWER
0 How old was Esther when she left school?	**A** 14		
	B 15		**C**
	C 16		

21   Why did Aunt Flory give Esther some money?

    A   Esther asked for it.
    B   Esther's friends needed it.
    C   It was a present.

22   After she left school, Esther

    A   went to college.
    B   started her own business.
    C   worked for her aunt.

23   Why did Esther make jam?

    A   She liked to eat it.
    B   She had a lot of fruit.
    C   She wanted to make money.

24   When Esther left school, her parents wanted her to

    A   go to college.
    B   be a businesswoman.
    C   work in a market.

25   Esther sold orange juice to

    A   the local market.
    B   a school.
    C   her friends.

26   Esther's parents were happy because Esther

    A   cooked for them.
    B   was busy.
    C   had a good business.

27   After two years, Esther

    A   paid people to help her.
    B   worked in a supermarket.
    C   opened a shop.

PART 5

QUESTIONS 28–35

Read the article about air travel.

Choose the best word (A, B or C) for each space (28–35).

For questions 28–35, mark A, B or C on the answer sheet.

A HISTORY OF AIR TRAVEL

In 1783, two French brothers built ......**0**...... first balloon to take people into the air. One hundred and twenty years later, in 1903, the Wright brothers built the first plane with an engine and ......**28**..... in it. This was ......**29**...... the United States. Then, in 1918, the US Post Office began the first airmail service.

Aeroplanes changed a ......**30**...... in the next thirty years. Then, in the 1950s, aeroplanes became much ......**31**...... because they had jet engines.

In 1976, Concorde was built in the UK and France. It is the fastest passenger plane in the world and it ......**32**...... fly at 2500 kilometres an hour, so the journey ......**33**....... London to New York is only four hours.

Today, millions of people travel ......**34**...... aeroplane, and it is difficult to think of a world without ......**35**....... .

EXAMPLE			ANSWER
0 A the	B a	C one	A
28 A fly	B flown	C flew	
29 A in	B at	C through	
30 A lot	B many	C few	
31 A fast	B faster	C fastest	
32 A must	B should	C can	
33 A between	B from	C of	
34 A with	B on	C by	
35 A them	B their	C they	

PART 6

QUESTIONS 36–40

Read the descriptions (36–40) of some holiday words.

What is the word for each description?

The first letter is already there. There is one space for each other letter in the word.

For questions 36–40, write the words on the answer sheet.

EXAMPLE	ANSWER
0 You may need this to leave the country.	*p a s s p o r t*

36 If you want a room in a hotel, you can phone and do this first.   *b __ __ __*

37 When you arrive at a hotel or a campsite, you go here first.   *r __ __ __ __ __ __ __*

38 You sleep inside this on a campsite.   *t __ __ __*

39 This kind of hotel room is for two people.   *d __ __ __ __ __*

40 You go here to enjoy the sun and swim in the sea.   *b __ __ __ __*

PART 7

QUESTIONS 41–50

Complete these letters.
Write ONE word for each space (41–50).
For questions 41–50, write your words on the answer sheet.

Dear Sir,

I lost (Example: ....*my*.... bag on a train ...**41**... week.
I was on the 8.30 a.m. train to Cambridge ...**42**...
10th May. It is ...**43**... large blue bag and my name
..**44**.. written on the outside. ...**45**... you found
this bag?

Yours faithfully,

Mary Johnson

Dear Ms Johnson,

I ...**46**... pleased to tell ...**47**... that we have your
bag here. If you come ...**48**... this office, ...**49**...
give it to you. The office ...**50**... at 9 a.m. and
closes at 6.30 p.m. every day.

Yours sincerely,

J Wilson

PART 8

QUESTIONS 51–55

Read the information about language courses and the e-mail message.
Fill in the information on the Course Booking Form.
For questions 51–55, write the information on the answer sheet.

Language Courses

French:	Monday evening
German:	Thursday evening
Portuguese:	Tuesday afternoon
Spanish:	Wednesday evening

Afternoon Classes: 2.30–4.30 p.m.
Evening Classes: 6.30–8.30 p.m.

To: International Language School

I come from Australia and I teach French to businessmen. I want to start learning Portuguese because next year I am going to work in Brazil. I am free after 1 p.m. on Tuesdays and Thursdays. Can I book a place on one of your courses?

Cheryl Harvey

International Language School
Course Booking Form

Full name:		*Cheryl Harvey*
Nationality:	**51**	
Occupation:	**52**	
Name of course:	**53**	
Day:	**54**	
Starting time:	**55**	

PART 9

QUESTION 56

Read this postcard from your friend, Alex.

POSTCARD

I am going to visit your country next month. Can I see you?

Please tell me about the weather there. What clothes should I bring?

Alex

Write a postcard to Alex.
Answer Alex's questions.

Write 25–35 words.
Write your postcard on the answer sheet.

PAPER 2 LISTENING (approximately 30 minutes including 8 minutes transfer time)

PART 1

QUESTIONS 1–5

You will hear five short conversations.

You will hear each conversation twice.

There is one question for each conversation.

For questions 1–5, put a tick ☑ under the right answer.

EXAMPLE

0 How many people were at the meeting?

3	13	30
A ☐	B ☐	C ☑

---

1 How will Mary travel to Scotland?

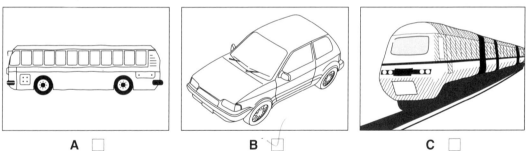

A ☐   B ☑   C ☐

2 Where are the shoes?

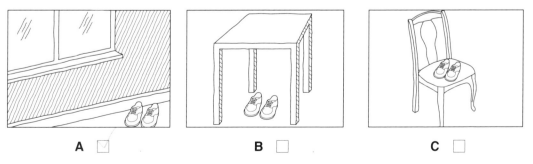

A ☑   B ☐   C ☐

3   When will the football match start next week?

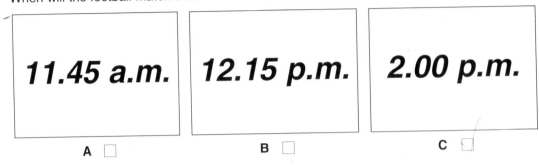

A ☐   B ☐   C ☑

4   Which box of chocolates do they buy?

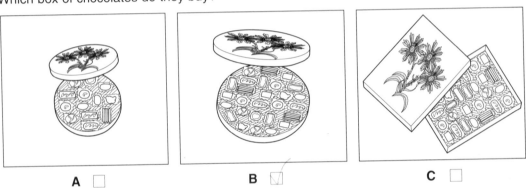

A ☐   B ☑   C ☐

5   When's Wendy's birthday?

A ☐   B ☑   C ☐

PART 2

QUESTIONS 6–10

Listen to Pete talking to a friend about his holiday.
What was the weather like each day?
For questions 6–10, write a letter A–H next to each day.
You will hear the conversation twice.

EXAMPLE	ANSWER
0 Monday	**B**

DAYS   **WEATHER**

6	Tuesday	☐	**A**	cloud
7	Wednesday	☐	**B**	cold
			C	fog
8	Thursday	☐	**D**	rain
9	Friday	☐	**E**	snow
			F	sun
10	Saturday	☐	**G**	warm
			H	wind

PART 3

QUESTIONS 11–15

Listen to Michael talking to Marina about a new sports centre.
For questions 11–15, tick ☑ A, B or C.
You will hear the conversation twice.

EXAMPLE				ANSWER
0 Where is the new sports centre?	**A**	Long Road		☑
	B	Bridge Street *near*	☐	
	C	Station Road	☐	

11 What sport **can't** you do at the sports centre?	**A**	tennis	☑
	B	table-tennis	☐
	C	volleyball	☐
12 How much must Marina pay?	**A**	£14 a year	☑
	B	£30 a year	☐
	C	£50 a year	☐
13 How many days a week is the sports centre open late?	**A**	2	☐
	B	3	☑
	C	4	☐
14 Which bus goes to the sports centre?	**A**	number 10	☐
	B	number 16	☑
	C	number 60	☐
15 When will Michael and Marina go to the sports centre?	**A**	Tuesday	☐
	B	Thursday	☐
	C	Friday	☐

PART 4

QUESTIONS 16–20

You will hear a conversation about a flat for rent.

Listen and complete questions 16–20.
You will hear the conversation twice.

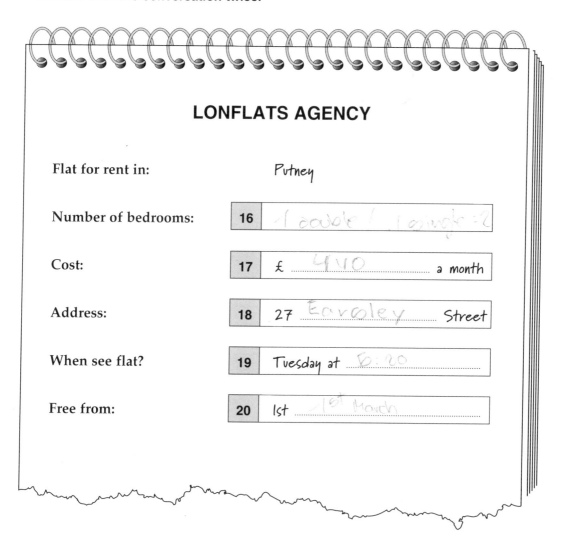

LONFLATS AGENCY

Flat for rent in: Putney

Number of bedrooms: 16 1 double / 1 single = 2

Cost: 17 £ 440 a month

Address: 18 27 Earsley Street

When see flat? 19 Tuesday at 6:20

Free from: 20 1st 1st March

PART 5

QUESTIONS 21–25

You will hear a tour guide talking about a day trip.

Listen and complete questions 21–25.

You will hear the information twice.

TRIP TO CHESTER	
Coach leaves:	9.15 a.m.
Arrives Chester:	**21** ~~11:45 a m~~
Morning visit:	**22** old building
Price of family ticket:	**23** £
Lunch in:	**24** 2 hours .
Afternoon visit:	**25** market

You now have 8 minutes to write your answers on the answer sheet.

PAPER 3   SPEAKING (8–10 minutes)

The Speaking test lasts 8–10 minutes. You will take the test with another candidate. There are two examiners, but only one of them will talk to you. The examiner will ask you questions and ask you to talk to the other candidate.

Part 1 (5–6 minutes)

The examiner will ask you and your partner some questions. These questions will be about your daily life, past experiences and future plans. For example, you may have to speak about your school, job, hobbies or home town.

Part 2 (3–4 minutes)

You and your partner will speak to each other. You will ask and answer questions. The examiner will give you a card with some information on it. The examiner will give your partner a card with some words on it. Your partner will use the words on the card to ask you questions about the information you have. Then you will change roles.

Test 3

PAPER 1 READING AND WRITING (1 hour 10 minutes)

PART 1

QUESTIONS 1–5

Which notice (A–H) says this (1–5)?
For questions 1–5, mark the correct letter A–H on the answer sheet.

EXAMPLE	ANSWER
0 Don't bring your dog in here.	F

1   These are cheaper if you buy several of them.

2   You can't get many different meals here.

3   Put this in a cold place.

4   You are too late to get a seat for this show.

5   This place is not open all night.

A   KEEP IN FRIDGE

B   Door locked at midnight – ask for key before going out.

C   SOUP AND HOT PIES ONLY

D   TICKETS FOR OASIS CONCERT ON SALE HERE *from 8 p.m.*

E   ALL THIS WEEK BUY 5 GET 1 FREE

F   NO ANIMALS IN RESTAURANT

G   ALL TICKETS SOLD

H   USE BY 19 JULY

PART 2

QUESTIONS 6–10

Read the sentences (6–10) about Lisa and her friend, Jane.
Choose the best word (A, B or C) for each space.
For questions 6–10, mark A, B or C on the answer sheet.

EXAMPLE   **ANSWER**

0 Lisa .... her friend Jane on the phone.   **C**

    A spoke   **B** talked   **C** called

---

6 'Let's get a video and .... it at my house this evening,' she said.

    A look   **B** watch   **C** listen

7 'That's a great .... !' said Jane. 'I've got nothing else to do.'

    A pity   **B** thing   **C** idea

8 They went to the video shop and .... a film with their favourite actor in it.

    A chose   **B** decided   **C** thought

9 Then they bought some .... of cola to drink and a big bag of sweets.

    A plates   **B** cups   **C** cans

10 They took everything back to Lisa's house and .... the film together.

    A enjoyed   **B** laughed   **C** liked

PART 3

QUESTIONS 11–15

Complete the five conversations.

For questions 11–15, mark A, B or C on the answer sheet.

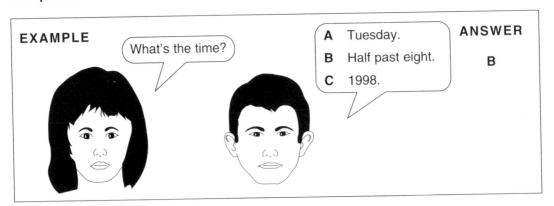

| EXAMPLE | What's the time? | A Tuesday.
 B Half past eight.
 C 1998. | ANSWER
 B |

11 Let's walk to the park.

    A All right.

    B I think so.

    C I'm sorry.

12 When did you arrive?

    A Tomorrow.

    B Yesterday.

    C For two days.

13 Shall I open the window?

    A Yes, I shall.

    B Yes, you will.

    C Yes, please.

14 I got a letter from Paul this morning.

    A I'm afraid not.

    B That's nice.

    C He's fine.

15 How's your sister?

    A She's Jane.

    B She's at school.

    C She's very well.

QUESTIONS 16–20

Complete the conversation.
What does the tourist say to the shop assistant?
For questions 16–20, mark the correct letter A–H on the answer sheet.

EXAMPLE		ANSWER
Assistant:	Good morning. Can I help you?	
Tourist:	0	D

Assistant:	For children or adults?	**A**	I'll take the cheaper one.
Tourist:	**16**		
Assistant:	A lot of tourists buy this one.	**B**	Oh, it's for me. I want a guide book.
Tourist:	**17**		
Assistant:	What about this one with fewer pages?	**C**	I haven't got any children.
Tourist:	**18**	**D**	Yes, please. I'd like a book about London.
Assistant:	The hardback is £8, and the paperback £3.50.	**E**	No, thank you. I want to use it now.
Tourist:	**19**		
Assistant:	Fine. Shall I put it in a bag for you?	**F**	That's very heavy. Have you got a smaller one?
Tourist:	**20**		
Assistant:	Here you are. Thank you.	**G**	Is it a good book?
Tourist:	Thanks. Goodbye.		
		H	That looks better. How much is it?

PART 4

QUESTIONS 21–27

Read the article about a young woman and then answer the questions.
For questions 21–27, mark A, B or C on the answer sheet.

REBECCA STEVENS

Rebecca Stevens was the first woman to climb Mount Everest. Before she went up the highest mountain in the world, she was a journalist and lived in a small flat in south London.

In 1993, Rebecca left her job and her family and travelled to Asia with some other climbers. She found that life on Everest is hard. 'You must carry everything on your back,' she explained, 'so you can only take things that you will need. You can't wash on the mountain, and in the end I didn't even take a toothbrush. I am usually a clean person but there is no water, only snow. Water is very heavy so you only take enough to drink!'

When Rebecca reached the top of Mount Everest on May 17 1993, it was the best moment of her life. Suddenly she became famous.

Now she has written a book about the trip and people often ask her to talk about it. She has a new job too, on a science programme on television.

Rebecca is well known today and she has more money, but she still lives in the little flat in south London among her pictures and books about mountains!

EXAMPLE			ANSWER
0 Everest is a	**A**	country.	**B**
	B	mountain.	
	C	town.	

21 Before Rebecca climbed Everest, she worked for

    A a bookshop.

    B a newspaper.

    C a travel agent.

22 Rebecca went to Everest

    A with her family.

    B with a climbing group.

    C without anyone.

23 Rebecca didn't take much luggage because she

    A didn't have many things.

    B had a bad back.

    C had to carry it herself.

24 Rebecca didn't wash on Everest because

    A it was too cold.

    B there was not enough water.

    C she is a dirty person.

25 Rebecca carried water for

    A drinking.

    B cooking.

    C cleaning her teeth.

26 Rebecca became famous when she

    A got to the highest place in the world.

    B wrote a book about her trip.

    C was on a television programme.

27 After her trip, Rebecca

    A earned the same money.

    B stayed in the same flat.

    C did the same job.

PART 5

QUESTIONS 28–35

Read the article about the ostrich.
Choose the best word (A, B or C) for each space (28–35).
For questions 28–35, mark A, B or C on the answer sheet.

THE OSTRICH

The ostrich is the ......**0**...... bird in the world, and
an adult can be more .....**28**..... 90 kilos. Most wild
ostriches live .....**29**..... southern Africa, but there are
only a .....**30**..... of them left. Like all birds, ostriches have wings, ...**31**.....
they cannot fly. They use .....**32**..... wings to help them turn when they
are running. Ostriches can run very fast, from 65 to 90 kilometres
.....**33**...... hour, so it is very difficult .....**34**..... other animals to catch them.

   Baby ostriches are the same size as chickens and take about 3 years
to become adults. Ostriches .....**35**..... plants and can live for many days
without water.

EXAMPLE			ANSWER
0 A large	**B** larger	**C** largest	C

28	**A** than	**B** of	**C** like
29	**A** on	**B** in	**C** at
30	**A** few	**B** little	**C** lot
31	**A** or	**B** and	**C** but
32	**A** them	**B** their	**C** its
33	**A** a	**B** an	**C** one
34	**A** for	**B** to	**C** by
35	**A** ate	**B** eats	**C** eat

PART 6

QUESTIONS 36–40

Read the descriptions (36–40) of some things you can find in a house.

What is the word for each description?

The first letter is already there. There is one space for each other letter in the word.

For questions 36–40, write the words on the answer sheet.

EXAMPLE	ANSWER
0 You sleep in this at night.	b _e_ _d_

36 People sit round this to eat their meals.   t _ _ _ _

37 You can keep your clothes in this.   c _ _ _ _ _ _ _

38 You wash yourself with soap and water in this.   s _ _ _ _ _

39 You look through this to see outside.   w _ _ _ _ _

40 People often put books or flowers on this.   s _ _ _ _

PART 7

QUESTIONS 41–50

Complete these letters.
Write ONE word for each space (41–50).
For questions 41–50, write your words on the answer sheet.

Dear Jacqueline,

Would you (Example: ...*like*...) to come ...**41**... the cinema ...**42**... me after school today? We can go to see *Pocahontas* at the ABC cinema. The film starts ...**43**... 6 o'clock. Shall ...**44**... meet outside the cinema?

    Love,

    Isabella

Dear Isabella,

I am very sorry but I can't go to the cinema ...**45**... evening. My mother has ...**46**... work, and I ...**47**... going to cook dinner.

Why don't you ...**48**... Karen to go? I hope ...**49**... like the film. You can tell me ...**50**... it tomorrow.

    Love,

    Jacqueline

PART 8

QUESTIONS 51–55

Read the letter and the information about Mr Ando, who is staying at a hotel in Leeds.

Fill in the Hotel Registration Form.
For questions 51–55, write the information on the answer sheet.

Grange Hotel, Leeds

Sunday 14 April

Dear Joe,

We like Oxford and I love my job there. We're renting a nice house at 23 Mount Road. We arrived in Leeds yesterday and will go back to Oxford tomorrow. I am here for a meeting and my wife, Keiko, has come too. She has a job as a teacher in Oxford. We will return to Japan next year.

Yours,

Toshi

OXFORD WORLD COMPUTERS
Toshi Ando
Engineer

Date and place of birth: 12.03.76
                                Tokyo, Japan

Married, no children

HOTEL REGISTRATION FORM

Name:		*Toshi Ando*
UK address:	**51**	
Nationality:	**52**	
Occupation:	**53**	
Name of wife/husband:	**54**	
Leaving date:	**55**	

PART 9

QUESTION 56

You are going to have a party. Write a note to a friend:

– **Ask** your friend to come.
– **Say when** and **where** the party is.

Write 25–35 words.
Write your note on the answer sheet.

PAPER 2 LISTENING (approximately 30 minutes including 8 minutes transfer time)

PART 1

QUESTIONS 1–5

You will hear five short conversations.

You will hear each conversation twice.

There is one question for each conversation.

For questions 1–5, put a tick ✓ under the right answer.

EXAMPLE

0   When's the school trip?

Tuesday	Wednesday	Thursday
A ☐	B ☐	C ✓

---

1   Where's the sports centre?

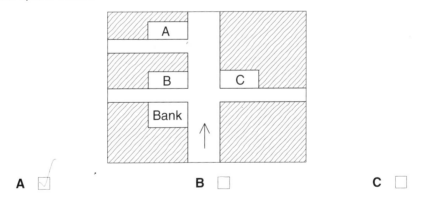

A ☑   B ☐   C ☐

2   How much petrol does the woman want?

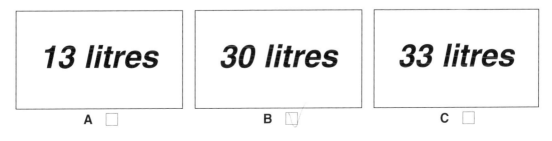

13 litres   **30 litres**   **33 litres**

A ☐   B ☑   C ☐

3 Which table do they buy?

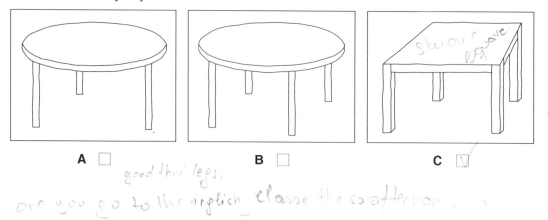

A ☐   B ☐   C ☑

good thri legs.

are you go to the inglich classe the so afternon.

4 What time does the class start?

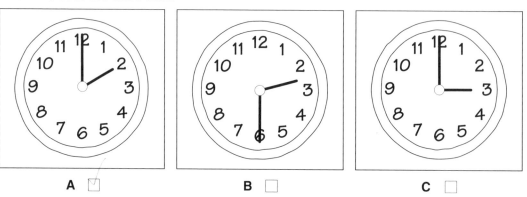

A ☑   B ☐   C ☐

5 What was the weather like on Emma's holiday?

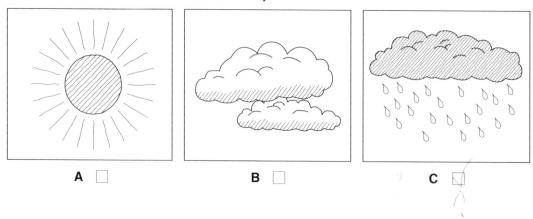

A ☐   B ☐   C ☑

PART 2

QUESTIONS 6–10

Listen to Jane talking to a friend about some clothes that she has bought for her holiday.

What colours are her clothes?

For questions 6–10, write a letter A–H next to each of her clothes.
You will hear the conversation twice.

EXAMPLE	ANSWER
0 shirt	H

CLOTHES		COLOURS	
6 dress	D	A	black
7 jacket	C	B	blue
		C	brown
8 sweater	E	D	green
9 coat	A	E	grey
10 shoes	D	F	orange
		G	red
		H	white

PART 3

QUESTIONS 11–15

Listen to Mrs Lee talking to her secretary about her business trip.
For questions 11–15, tick ☑ A, B or C.
You will hear the conversation twice.

EXAMPLE			ANSWER
0 Mrs Lee will leave on	**A**	Friday.	☐
	B	Saturday.	☑
	C	Sunday.	☐

11 Mrs Lee's plane goes at	**A**	8 a.m.	☑
	B	10 a.m.	☐
	C	11 a.m.	☐
12 She is going to	**A**	Amsterdam.	☐
	B	Frankfurt.	☐
	C	London.	☑
13 First she will go to	**A**	a factory.	☑
	B	an office.	☐
	C	a hotel.	☐
14 She will have dinner in	**A**	a restaurant.	☐
	B	her hotel.	☐
	C	someone's house.	☐
15 The next morning she will travel by	**A**	plane.	☐
	B	train.	☑
	C	car.	☐

PART 4

QUESTIONS 16–20

You will hear a man asking for some information about a language school.

Listen and complete questions 16–20.
You will hear the conversation twice.

School of Italian Studies

Length of courses:	*6 or 9 months*
Next course begins on:	**16** Next Monday.
Number of students in each class:	**17** 15
Cost of coursebook:	**18** £ 12,99
School hours:	
Monday to Friday:	*From: 8 a.m. to: 7 p.m.*
Saturday:	**19** *From:* 9 a.m. *to:* 1 p.m.
Nearest underground station:	**20** Green Park

PART 5

QUESTIONS 21–25

You will hear a man talking about a day trip.

Listen and complete questions 21–25.

You will hear the information twice.

DAY TRIP

Leave:	*9.30* a.m.
Trip will take:	**21** .... *7* .... hours
We will stop at three places:	
Stop 1:	**22** *Castle*
Stop 2:	**23** *Cafe* at 1 o'clock
Stop 3:	**24** *Beach*
Take your:	**25** *camera* .

You now have 8 minutes to write your answers on the answer sheet.

PAPER 3 SPEAKING (8–10 minutes)

The Speaking test lasts 8–10 minutes. You will take the test with another candidate. There are two examiners, but only one of them will talk to you. The examiner will ask you questions and ask you to talk to the other candidate.

Part 1 (5–6 minutes)

The examiner will ask you and your partner some questions. These questions will be about your daily life, past experiences and future plans. For example, you may have to speak about your school, job, hobbies or home town.

Part 2 (3–4 minutes)

You and your partner will speak to each other. You will ask and answer questions. The examiner will give you a card with some information on it. The examiner will give your partner a card with some words on it. Your partner will use the words on the card to ask you questions about the information you have. Then you will change roles.

Test 4

PAPER 1   READING AND WRITING (1 hour 10 minutes)

PART 1

QUESTIONS 1–5

Which notice (A–H) says this (1–5)?

For questions 1–5, mark the correct letter A–H on the answer sheet.

EXAMPLE	ANSWER
0 You can sleep here.	F

1   You must not play football here.

2   You may be late.

3   You should not leave your car here.

4   You can study here soon.

5   You cannot drive here today.

A   **Bridge closed to traffic because of high wind.**

B   DELAYS POSSIBLE

C   OLYMPIC SPORTS CENTRE – use your student card here.

D   DO NOT PARK IN FRONT OF THE GARAGE

E   CAR PARK £2.00 for 2 hours

F   GUEST HOUSE

G   NO BALL GAMES ON GRASS

H   COMPUTER COURSE STARTS ON MONDAY.

PART 2

QUESTIONS 6–10

Read the sentences (6–10) about cooking.
Choose the best word (A, B or C) for each space.
For questions 6–10, mark A, B or C on the answer sheet.

EXAMPLE	ANSWER
0 Claudia was going to cook a .... for her parents.	**B**
A food **B** meal **C** plate	

6 She .... some fruit and vegetables from the market.

    A bought   **B** kept   **C** grew

7 She cut up some meat and onions and fried them in a pan on the ....

    A cooker   **B** cupboard   **C** fridge

8 There was a big .... of salad to eat afterwards.

    A bottle   **B** bowl   **C** spoon

9 When everything was .... they all sat down at the table.

    A real   **B** round   **C** ready

10 After dinner, Claudia's parents .... her to wash up.

    A practised   **B** agreed   **C** helped

PART 3

QUESTIONS 11–15

Complete the five conversations.

For questions 11–15, mark A, B or C on the answer sheet.

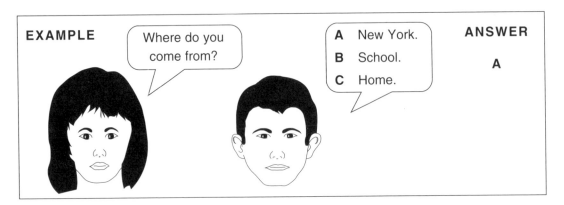

EXAMPLE	Where do you come from?	A New York.
		B School.
		C Home.

ANSWER

A

11   How far is it to Manchester?

    A   About two months.

    B   It's quite long.

    C   Almost 30 kilometres.

12   Could you give me the butter?

    A   Here you are.

    B   Thank you.

    C   I don't know.

13   John hates shopping.

    A   I love it.

    B   It's six pounds.

    C   The shop's open.

14   I've already done my homework.

    A   When did you do it?

    B   Please do it.

    C   Have you done it yet?

15   What's the date today?

    A   It's Thursday.

    B   The third, I think.

    C   I'm 22 today.

EXAMPLE		ANSWER
0 Nicola's first job was	**A** at a college	
	B with Saudi Arabian Airlines	**C**
	C at a local airport.	

21   When Nicola first started working for British Airways, she was

A   a manager.

B   an air hostess.

C   a pilot.

22   Nicola does most of her work

A   in the office.

B   in aeroplanes.

C   in meetings.

23   Most days, Nicola starts work at

A   8 a.m.

B   1 p.m.

C   4 p.m.

24   At the beginning of each day, Nicola

A   goes to a meeting.

B   talks to air hostesses.

C   works with her computer.

25   What does Nicola like best?

A   flying

B   working in the office

C   helping people

26   The first thing Nicola does after a long journey is

A   go to bed.

B   have a meal.

C   go to the office.

27   Nicola would like to

A   stay in the same job.

B   stop travelling.

C   earn more money.

PART 5

QUESTIONS 28–35

Read the article about a working holiday.

Choose the best word (A, B or C) for each space (28–35).

For questions 28–35, mark A, B or C on the answer sheet.

The Ruwenzori Mountains

Mary Daniels is a student in England. This year she ......**0**...... a very interesting summer holiday. She travelled ......**28**..... fifteen other people to the Ruwenzori Mountains in Africa. They went there to help make a road ......**29**...... a forest between two big towns. 'It was very difficult ......**30**...... there was no water to drink and no shops where we ......**31**...... buy food,' said Mary. 'It was also very cold and wet in the mountains. It is ......**32**...... of the wettest places in the world.'

Mary stayed in the mountains ......**33**...... six weeks. It was hard work, but she says it was the ......**34**...... thing she has ever ......**35**...... . She is hoping to return next year to do some more work there.

EXAMPLE			ANSWER
0 **A** had	**B** have	**C** has	**A**

28	**A** to	**B** with	**C** by
29	**A** through	**B** on	**C** among
30	**A** so	**B** because	**C** why
31	**A** could	**B** must	**C** may
32	**A** one	**B** some	**C** any
33	**A** for	**B** during	**C** since
34	**A** good	**B** best	**C** better
35	**A** did	**B** do	**C** done

PART 6

QUESTIONS 36–40

Read the descriptions (36–40) of some clothes.

What is the word for each description?

The first letter is already there. There is one space for each other letter in the word.

For questions 36–40, write the words on the answer sheet.

EXAMPLE	ANSWER
0 You put this on your head.	h _a_ _t_

36 These are often made of leather and you wear them on your feet.   s _ _ _ _

37 This is a jacket and trousers in the same colour.   s _ _ _

38 This will keep you dry in wet weather.   r _ _ _ _ _ _ _

39 When the weather is too hot for long trousers, men and
women often wear these with a T-shirt.   s _ _ _ _ _

40 You can put this on over a T-shirt if you feel cold.   s _ _ _ _ _ _

PART 7

QUESTIONS 41–50

Complete the letter.

Write ONE word for each space (41–50).

For questions 41–50, write your words on the answer sheet.

Dear Mike,

I am sorry you (Example: _could_) not come to my party yesterday. Jon __41__ me you had a very bad cold and you __42__ to stay in bed. __43__ you feeling better now?

It was __44__ very good party; __45__ nicest I have ever had! Lots of my friends __46__ there and they gave __47__ some lovely presents. I will tell __48__ more about the party when you come __49__ school __50__ Monday.

Love,

Lorenzo

PART 8

QUESTIONS 51–55

Read the travel information and the letter.

Fill in the information on the Luggage Report Form.

For questions 51–55, write the information on the answer sheet.

<table>
<tr><td colspan="3" align="center">**Travel Information for** Kevin Brown</td></tr>
<tr><td align="center">**Date**</td><td align="center">**Leave**</td><td align="center">**Arrive**</td></tr>
<tr><td align="center">14 May</td><td align="center">Boston 21.45</td><td align="center">Paris 22.05</td></tr>
<tr><td align="center">21 May</td><td align="center">Paris 14.15</td><td align="center">Boston 18.25</td></tr>
</table>

Luggage: not more than 20 **kilos**

Enjoy your trip!
Air America

---

22 May

Air America
Boston Airport

Dear Sir,

Yesterday I returned from Paris. When I got my suitcase back at the airport it was broken and there is black oil on my clothes. I should like some money for a new suitcase and some new clothes.

Kevin Brown

LUGGAGE REPORT FORM

Passenger's name: *Kevin Brown*

Date of journey: **51** _____

Flying from: **52** _____

Time flight arrived: **53** _____

How much luggage did you have?   **54** _____

What was in it?   **55** _____

PART 9

QUESTION 56

Your friend, Chris, has got your cassette recorder. Now you need it.

Write a note to Chris:

– **Ask** for the cassette recorder.
– **Say why** and **when** you need it.

Write 25–35 words.
Write your note on the answer sheet.

PAPER 2 LISTENING (approximately 30 minutes including 8 minutes transfer time)

PART 1

QUESTIONS 1–5

You will hear five short conversations.

You will hear each conversation twice.

There is one question for each conversation.

For questions 1–5, put a tick ☑ under the right answer.

EXAMPLE

0   What time is it?

06.00	08.00	09.00
A ☐	**B** ☐	**C** ☑

1   What was the weather like on Wednesday?

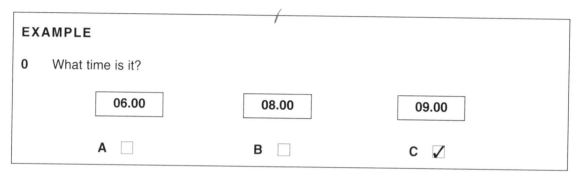

A ☐   B ☑   C ☐

2   How much did Mark's pullover cost?

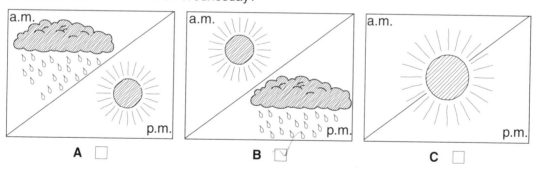

A ☐   B ☐   C ☐

3   What did Raquel buy today?

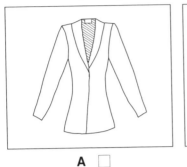   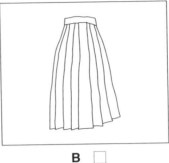   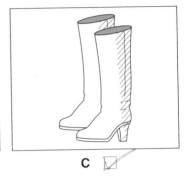

A ☐   B ☐   C ☑

4   How many students are there at the college?

A ☐   B ☐   C ☑

5   What is David going to buy?

      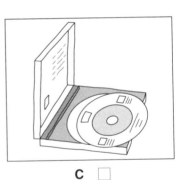

A ☑   B ☐   C ☐

PART 2

QUESTIONS 6–10

Listen to Philip talking to his mother about his son, Simon.
What is Simon going to do on Saturday and Sunday?
For questions 6–10, write a letter A–H next to each time of day.
You will hear the conversation twice.

EXAMPLE	ANSWER
0 Saturday morning	C

TIMES

6   Saturday afternoon

7   Saturday evening

8   Sunday morning

9   Sunday afternoon

10   Sunday evening

ACTIVITIES

A   bicycle ride

B   football match

C   judo class

D   party

E   swimming

F   the cinema

G   the park

H   watching television

PART 3

QUESTIONS 11–15

Listen to Chloe talking to a man about a sailing holiday.

For questions 11–15, tick ✓ A, B or C.
You will hear the conversation twice.

EXAMPLE			ANSWER
0 Chloe wants to go to	**A**	Italy.	✓
	B	Sweden.	☐
	C	Switzerland.	☐

11	How many times has Chloe been sailing before?	**A**	never	✓
		B	once	☐
		C	twice	☐
12	How much can Chloe spend?	**A**	£300	☐
		B	£380	✓
		C	£450	☐
13	Chloe will go in	**A**	August.	☐
		B	September.	☐
		C	October.	☐
14	Chloe would like to sail on	**A**	a lake.	✓
		B	the sea.	☐
		C	a river.	☐
15	How does Chloe want to pay?	**A**	by cheque	☐
		B	with cash	☐
		C	by credit card	✓

PART 4

QUESTIONS 16–20

You will hear Kate and Jeremy talking about a party.

Listen and complete questions 16–20.
You will hear the conversation twice.

Kate's Birthday Party

Kate will be:		17 years old
Day:	16	*Friday*
Time:	17	*8:30*
Place:	18	*London Hotel*
Address:	19	*Shandy* .... Street
Bring some:	20	*Pencils*

PART 5

QUESTIONS 21–25

You will hear some information about a cinema.

Listen and complete questions 21–25.

You will hear the information twice.

CINEMA

Name of cinema: North London Arts Cinema

Next week's film: **21** .... Moon light ..... Meeting

from: **22** Monday to .... Thursday ....

times: **23** 6.45 p.m. and .... 9:15 ....

Student ticket costs: **24** £ 2'80 .

Nearest car park: **25** .... Hoxton .... Street

You now have 8 minutes to write your answers on the answer sheet.

PAPER 3   SPEAKING (8–10 minutes)

The Speaking test lasts 8–10 minutes. You will take the test with another candidate. There are two examiners, but only one of them will talk to you. The examiner will ask you questions and ask you to talk to the other candidate.

Part 1 (5–6 minutes)

The examiner will ask you and your partner some questions. These questions will be about your daily life, past experiences and future plans. For example, you may have to speak about your school, job, hobbies or home town.

Part 2 (3–4 minutes)

You and your partner will speak to each other. You will ask and answer questions. The examiner will give you a card with some information on it. The examiner will give your partner a card with some words on it. Your partner will use the words on the card to ask you questions about the information you have. Then you will change roles.

Visual materials for Paper 3

1A

Mary Brown

DENTIST

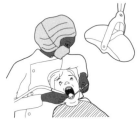

17, Mount Street

For appointments Tel: 980 4723

Opening times: Monday–Thursday 12.30–8 p.m.

Car parking in Water Lane

1D

NEW SHOPPING CENTRE

- ◆ name?

- ◆ where?

- ◆ many shops?

- ◆ car park?

- ◆ open today?

1B

DENTIST

- ◆ name?

- ◆ telephone number?

- ◆ appointment / evening?

- ◆ address?

- ◆ car park?

1C

WESTWOOD SHOPPING CENTRE

opens next month!

**10 kilometres from city centre
(<u>free</u> car park for 800 cars)**

**more than 100 shops,
2 restaurants, 4 cafés and a cinema**

2A

INTERNATIONAL LIBRARY

BOOKS, CDs
AND VIDEOS

OVER 100 FOREIGN
NEWSPAPERS AND
MAGAZINES

ENTRANCE FREE

Monday – Saturday 9.30 a.m. – 6 p.m.

New England House, Museum Street

2D

HOLIDAY SPORTS CLUB

◆ what sports?

◆ address?

◆ all ages?

◆ cost?   £

◆ when / open?

2B

LIBRARY

◆ where?

◆ close?

◆ open / Sunday?

◆ cost?   £

◆ foreign magazines?

2C

Holiday Sports Club

27 London Road

July – August
for young people (10–18 years)

Play a different sport every day
(football, basketball, volleyball, tennis and baseball)

Price £25 a week

3A

SILVER LAKE

A great place for a holiday

20 kilometres from the city airport
5 large, new hotels
Walking, swimming and boat trips
Dry and sunny 300 days a year

3D

ISLAND

◆ **name / island?**

◆ **what / see?**

◆ **where / stay?**

◆ **weather?**

◆ **how / get there?**

3B

LAKE

- name / lake?

- where?

- rain / often?

- what / do?

- modern hotels?

3C

RED SANDS ISLAND

A beautiful island for a special holiday

Sun and blue sky

Hundreds of different birds
Campsite for 50 tents

Boats daily from Port Martin

4A

SANDON AIR MUSEUM

More than 70 aeroplanes to look at
OPEN DAILY   10 a.m. – 6 p.m.
Shop with books and postcards
Large free car park

Tickets: Adults £8.00   Students £5.00

4D

BOOKSHOP

◆ **address ?**

◆ **big / small ?**

◆ **closed / Sundays ?**

◆ **sell / travel books ?**

◆ **telephone / number ?**

4B

MUSEUM

- ◆ **what / see ?**

- ◆ **open / weekends ?**

- ◆ **student ticket? £**

- ◆ **car park ?**

- ◆ **buy postcard?**

4C

WORLD BOOKS

212 Main Street

Largest bookshop in the country

Get your travel books here

Monday–Saturday	10.00 a.m. – 8.00 p.m.
Sunday	12.30 p.m. – 8.00 p.m.

Tel: 724 399

Test 1 Key

Paper 1 Reading and Writing

Part 1
1 H   2 F   3 E   4 A   5 G

Part 2
6 B   7 C   8 C   9 A   10 B

Part 3
11 C   12 B   13 A   14 B   15 C
16 B   17 A   18 F   19 H   20 C

Part 4
21 A   22 C   23 B   24 C   25 B   26 B   27 A

Part 5
28 A   29 B   30 A   31 C   32 A   33 B   34 B   35 B

Part 6
For questions 36–40, spelling must be correct.
36 uncle   37 grandmother   38 wife   39 aunt   40 daughter

Part 7
For questions 41–50, ignore capitals/absence of capitals. Spelling must be correct.
41 in   42 like   43 much   44 how   45 you   46 on/from
47 costs/is/'s   48 to   49 a/one/our/the/another   50 this/that/it

Part 8
For questions 51–55, spelling must be correct and capitals must be used where necessary.
51 (Mr etc.) (SJ) Renshaw   52 (on/from) 10(th) April
53 (for) 7/seven days/a/one week   54 Mary Jones
55 22 King's Road, Weston

Part 9
Question 56
The note should include the following three pieces of information:

i   reason why can't go
ii mention of meeting on another day
iii where you can meet on another day.

Sample answer A

Mark: 5

The three parts of the message are clearly communicated and there are only occasional grammatical errors (*go to the swimming*).

> Dear Lina,
> I am sorry I can't because I go to the cinema. Can we go to the swimming on Sunday at 6.30 in the evening. If you want to go. come to the bus station on Sunday at 6.00 o'clock.
> See you later
> Yours Shida

Sample answer B

Mark: 4

All three parts of the message are communicated but more frequent errors in the structure prevent it from achieving a 5.

> I am sorry Penny for the swimming tomorrows evening. My grandmother she is in the hospital. It's possible for me at Saturday night. We go at disco.
> Celia

Sample answer C

Mark: 3

The writer has attempted all three parts of the task but the confusion of tense, *viseted*, and use of *last week* rather than *next week* requires interpretation on the part of the reader.

> I'm Sorry my friend. I cant go with you Because I viseted My grand Mother and grand father. Can you meet Last week.
> See my soon
> Ali

Sample answer D

Mark: 1

The writer has only covered one part of the message. There are also many errors in both the spelling and the grammar.

> *Dear, Mohan*
> *I'am sory I can not tomorrow go to the sea For swimming.*
> *I'am ill. Now I'am sleep in Hospital. I'am good helth*

Sample answer E

Mark: 0

This is an example of a candidate either not understanding or not following the task.

> *Dear Andre.*
> *Hi I am sorry I don't understand you why you can't go weth me to*
> *Leeds. Do you know when you can go weth me becaus I whant buy*
> *bots call me please.*
> *see you letter by.*

Paper 2   Listening

Part 1
1 B   **2** C   **3** B   **4** B   **5** C

Part 2
6 E   **7** F   **8** A   **9** C   **10** G

Part 3
11 A   **12** C   **13** A   **14** B   **15** A

Part 4
For questions 16–20, ignore capitals/absence of capitals. In question 16, spelling must be correct. For questions 17–20, accept recognisable spelling.
16 HYDE   **17** factory   **18** 11.30/half past eleven/eleven thirty
19 21/twenty-one   **20** photograph(s)/photo(s)

Part 5
For questions 21, 24 and 25, accept recognisable spelling. Spelling of car park *and* pink *needs to be correct.*
21 7.30/half past seven/seven thirty   **22** (big) car park (behind hotel)
23 pink   **24** (the) office   **25** (a) jacket

Transcript

This is the Key English Test. Paper 2. Listening. Test number one. There are five parts to the test. Parts One, Two, Three, Four and Five.

We will now stop for a moment before we start the test. Please ask any questions now because you mustn't speak during the test.

[pause]

PART 1   *Look at the instructions for Part One.*

[pause]

You will hear five short conversations.
You will hear each conversation twice.
There is one question for each conversation.
For questions 1–5, put a tick under the right answer.

Here is an example:
How many people were at the meeting?

Woman: Were there many people at the meeting?
Man: About thirty.
Woman: That's not many.
Man: No, but more than last time.

[pause]

The answer is 30, so there is a tick in box C.
Now we are ready to start.
Look at question one.

[pause]

Question 1   *One*

What will they eat for dinner this evening?

Mother: What do you want for dinner this evening, Maria? We could have pizza
                … or chicken.
Maria: Mm, what about fish? I had a pizza last night.
Mother: OK. That's easy to cook.
Maria: Good.

[pause]

Now listen again.

[pause]

[repeat]

[pause]

Question 2   *Two*
What time is it?

Man: Have you got the right time? I think my watch is wrong.
Woman: Er – it's half past two.
Man: Ah – my watch says twenty past.
Woman   Well, it's ten minutes slow then.

[pause]

Now listen again.

[repeat]

[pause]

Question 3   *Three*

What's Michelle going to read?

Man: Can I read your newspaper, Michelle?
Michelle: Didn't you bring a book with you?
Man: Yes, but it's not very interesting.
Michelle: Oh, here you are. I'll read this letter from John.

[pause]

Now listen again.

[repeat]

[pause]

Question 4   *Four*

How much did the tickets cost?

Woman: Oh hi – did you have a good time at the theatre last night?
Man: Well, the play was excellent but the tickets cost ninety dollars each.
Woman: That's not too bad if the play was good.
Man: No, perhaps you're right.

[pause]

Now listen again.

[repeat]

[pause]

Question 5   *Five*

Where is the chemist's?

Man: Excuse me, can you tell me where the chemist's is, please?
Woman: Mm, just a moment. Oh yes! It's past the post office, next to a big
                supermarket.
Man: Is it far from here?
Woman: No, just two minutes' walk.

[pause]

Now listen again.

[repeat]

[pause]

This is the end of Part One.

Now look at Part Two.

[pause]

PART 2 *Listen to Kate telling Emma about her family.*
Where is each person going today?
For questions 6–10, write a letter, A–H, next to each person.
You will hear the conversation twice.

[pause]

Emma: Hi, Kate. What about a game of tennis some time?
Kate: I'd like to Emma, but not today. I'm really busy.
Emma: What are you doing?
Kate: Sam's got toothache so I'm going to take him to the dentist this morning …
Emma: Oh dear!
Kate: … and then mother's going to the hairdresser this afternoon and I said I would drive her home afterwards. Then after school Tanya wants me to help her buy some new shoes. She doesn't like shopping alone.
Emma: My daughter doesn't either. You're going to the concert this evening, aren't you?
Kate: I'm afraid not. But Len loves classical music, so he'll go.
Emma: Oh good. By the way, has Tom started driving yet?
Kate: He's having his first lesson today. He's going to the driving school at lunchtime. He's really excited about it.
Emma: I'm sure he is. How's your father? Does he still play golf?
Kate: No, not any more, but he's started learning Spanish. Actually, he's got a class this evening!
Emma: Good for him. Well, perhaps we can go to the tennis club tomorrow?
Kate: Yes, OK!

[pause]

Now listen again.

[repeat]

[pause]

This is the end of Part Two.
Now look at Part Three.

[pause]

PART 3 *Listen to a woman talking to a policeman.*
For questions 11–15, tick A, B or C.
You will hear the conversation twice.
Look at questions 11–15 now. You have 20 seconds.

[pause]

Now listen to the conversation.

Man: Good morning, madam. Can I help you?
Woman: Yes. I've lost my bag.
Man: Oh, I am sorry. Now, where did you lose it?
Woman: In the town centre. I had it when I got off the bus.
Man: Was there much money in the bag?
Woman: No, there wasn't. I usually have forty or fifty pounds in it, but today I think there was only about twenty.
Man: What else was in the bag?

Woman: Just my gloves. I left my credit card and driving licence at home.

Man: Was the bag expensive?

Woman: No, it was an old one. It wasn't big enough really.

Man: Now, what time did you lose it?

Woman: Well, I left home about nine thirty and the bus takes half an hour, so I lost it about ten o'clock.

Man: Right. Well, I'll phone you tomorrow to tell you if we find it. Are you at home in the afternoon?

Woman: Sorry, I'm going out until the evening. Could you phone before ten in the morning?

Man: Certainly. I'll call then. Now, what's your number?

Woman: It's oh three six two …

[pause]

Now listen again.

[repeat]

[pause]

This is the end of Part Three.
Now look at Part Four.

[pause]

PART 4   *You will hear a man speaking on the telephone.*
He wants to speak to Miss Dixon, but she's not there.
Listen and complete questions 16–20.
You will hear the conversation twice.

[pause]

Woman: Brown's Builders, good afternoon.

Man: Good afternoon. I'd like to speak to Miss Dixon, please.

Woman: I'm afraid she's not in the office at the moment.

Man: Can you give her a message for me?

Woman: Yes, certainly. Who's calling please?

Man: My name is Hyde.

Woman: How do you spell that, please?

Man: That's H-Y-D-E.

Woman: Right, Mr Hyde.

Man: Could you tell her that the time of the meeting has changed?

Woman: Is that the meeting about the new houses?

Man: No, about the new factory.

Woman: I see. And when is it?

Man: It's on Wednesday at half past eleven.

Woman: Does Miss Dixon know where the meeting is?

Man: I think so. It's in our main office. Ask her to go to Room 21.

Woman: Right, I'll tell her.

Man: And could you ask her to bring the photographs with her?

Woman: Which photos do you mean?

Man: She'll know which ones. They're very important.

Woman: Don't worry, I'll tell her. Thank you very much, Mr Hyde.

Man: Thank you. Goodbye.

Woman: Goodbye.

[pause]

Now listen again.

[repeat]

[pause]

This is the end of Part Four.
Now look at Part Five.

[pause]

PART 5   *You will hear a man talking about a day trip.*
Listen and complete questions 21–25.
You will hear the information twice.

[pause]

Tour guide: Ladies and gentlemen. Here's some information about our trip to Loch Ness tomorrow. It's a long journey, about three hours each way, so we have to start early. That means we'll have breakfast at half past seven. Don't be late, please, as the bus has to leave at half past eight. When you finish breakfast, go to the car park. That's where we'll get on the bus. That's the big car park behind the hotel. Remember to bring your pink tickets for lunch. We'll have lunch at a restaurant near Loch Ness and you must have your pink ticket or you won't get any lunch! If you haven't got a pink ticket yet, you can get one from the office.

Oh, one more thing. I know it's summer but it can get quite cold in the mountains even in July, so bring a jacket with you. You'll need one in the evening.

All right? I'll see you tomorrow morning.

[pause]

Now listen again.

[repeat]

[pause]

This is the end of Part Five.

You now have eight minutes to write your answers on the answer sheet.

Note: Teacher, stop the recording here and time eight minutes.
Remind students when there is **one** minute remaining.

[pause]

This is the end of the test.

Test 2 Key

Paper 1 Reading and Writing

Part 1
1 D   2 A   3 C   4 B   5 E

Part 2
6 C   7 B   8 C   9 B   10 A

Part 3
11 C   12 B   13 A   14 B   15 C
16 C   17 E   18 G   19 B   20 A

Part 4
21 C   22 B   23 C   24 A   25 B   26 C   27 A

Part 5
28 C   29 A   30 A   31 B   32 C   33 B   34 C   35 A

Part 6
Spelling must be correct.

36 book   37 reception   38 tent   39 double   40 beach

Part 7
For questions 41–50, ignore capitals/absence of capitals. Spelling must be correct.
41 last/this   42 on   43 a   44 is/was   45 have
46 am/'m   47 you   48 to   49 will/can/shall/'ll   50 opens

Part 8
For questions 51–55, spelling must be correct and capitals must be used where necessary.
51 Australian   52 teacher   53 Portuguese
54 Tuesday   55 2.30 p.m./14.30

Part 9
Question 56
The postcard should include the following three pieces of information:

i   whether they can see Alex
ii comment about the weather
iii suggestion re: clothes.

Sample answer A

Mark: 5

All three parts of the message are communicated but there are a few errors of spelling and grammar. This is an example of a script that only just merits 5 marks.

> *Hello. Thank you for your letter. Of corse, I want to see you too.*
> *Well, My country is very cold. So you should bring many sweaters,*
> *jeanse, coats etc. I think so!!*
> *Love, Lola*

Sample answer B

Mark: 4

All three parts of the message are communicated with no need for interpretation on the part of the reader, but there are too many errors in spelling and grammar to merit a 5.

> *Hello Alex*
> *Thinks for your postcard. I love to see you. can you came in my*
> *house. The weather of my country is hot than you need to bring*
> *summer clothes.*
> *Sunny*

Sample answer C

Mark: 3

All three parts of the message have been covered but *long clothes* needs interpretation.

> *Dear Alex:*
> *Next month you can come to England see me. In England is*
> *winter now. If you come to see me you bring long clothes.*
> *Love from Valerie*

Sample answer D

Mark: 2

Only two of the points are covered and the errors are such that a considerable amount of patience is required of the reader.

> *Der Alex you are wolle comme in may contry next month I am free*
> *The weather is Bioutifoule son chain evriday.*
> *Good bay*
> *Peter*

Sample answer E

Mark: 0

This candidate only attempts one of the three points (clothes) and therefore can only be given one mark. However, they have only written 23 words and so they lose one mark because the answer is too short. Hence, the final score is zero.

> *Dear Alex*
> *I received your letter written at the back of a beautiful postcard.*
> *And you need to bring heavy clothes.*
> *Love Thomas*

Paper 2   Listening

Part 1

1 B   **2** A   **3** C   **4** B   **5** B

Part 2

6 H   **7** F   **8** A   **9** D   **10** G

Part 3

11 A   **12** B   **13** B   **14** B   **15** C

Part 4

For questions 16–20, ignore capitals/absence of capitals. In questions 18, 19 and 20, spelling must be correct.

16 two/2/one double, one single   **17** 440(.00)   **18** E A R S L E Y

19 5.30/five thirty/half past five   **20** (of) March

Part 5

For all questions, accept recognisable spelling, except number 24. Ignore capitals/absence of capitals.

21 10.45/quarter to eleven   **22** castle   **23** 8(.00)

24 park   **25** (walk to/round the old) market(s)

Transcript

PART 1   *Look at the instructions for Part One.*

[pause]

You will hear five short conversations.
You will hear each conversation twice.
There is one question for each conversation.
For questions 1–5, put a tick under the right answer.

Here is an example:
How many people were at the meeting?

Woman: Were there many people at the meeting?
Man: About thirty.
Woman: That's not many.
Man: No, but more than last time.

[pause]

The answer is 30, so there is a tick in box C.
Now we are ready to start.
Look at question one.

[pause]

Question 1 *One*
How will Mary travel to Scotland?

John: Are you taking the train to Scotland tomorrow, Mary?
Mary: No, I'm driving there, it's cheaper.
John: Why don't you go by coach?
Mary: Oh no, it takes seven hours.

[pause]

Now listen again.

[repeat]

[pause]

Question 2   *Two*
Where are the shoes?

Peter: Mum, have you seen my brown shoes?
Mother: Yes, they're under the table.
Peter: No they're not. I left them on the chair this morning, but they're not there now.
Mother: There they are – under the window!

[pause]

93

Now listen again.

[repeat]

[pause]

Question 3   *Three*

When will the football match start next week?

Tom: Does the football match start at quarter past twelve every week?
Bill: No, it was early this week. It usually begins at 2 o'clock.
Tom: So, it'll be the usual time next week?
Bill: Yes.

[pause]

Now listen again.

[repeat]

[pause]

Question 4   *Four*

Which box of chocolates do they buy?

Boy: Which box of chocolates shall we get Mum for her birthday?
Girl: Those round boxes with the flowers on are nice.
Boy: Yes, but that square box is cheaper.
Girl: But it's Mum's birthday. Let's get the big round one – we've got enough money!

Boy: OK.

[pause]

Now listen again.

[repeat]

[pause]

Question 5   *Five*

When's Wendy's birthday?

John: Wendy, you're twenty-one on Saturday, aren't you?
Wendy: No, my birthday's on May the eighteenth.
John: Well, Saturday is the eighteenth.
Wendy: No, it's not, it's the sixteenth.

[pause]

Now listen again.

[repeat]

[pause]

This is the end of Part One.

Now look at Part Two.

[pause]

PART 2   *Listen to Pete talking to a friend about his holiday.*
What was the weather like each day?
For questions 6–10, write a letter, A–H, next to each day.
You will hear the conversation twice.

[pause]

Helen: Hi Pete – you're looking well.
Pete: Yes, I've just been on holiday in the mountains for a week.
Helen: You must have had good weather.
Pete: Well, not really. When I arrived on the Monday it was very cold.
Helen: It can be cold in the mountains at this time of the year.
Pete: Yes – it wasn't very nice really. Then, on Tuesday it was so windy I just stayed in the hotel all day.
Helen: Did the weather get better?
Pete: Well, Wednesday was a bit better. There wasn't any wind and it was sunny most of the day.
Helen: So did you do a lot of walking?
Pete: No. By Thursday it was very cloudy and it looked as if it was going to snow.
Helen: And did it?
Pete: No, but on Friday it rained a lot.
Helen: And what about your last day?
Pete: Well, the weather was getting better and it was quite warm then. But it was a bit too late.

[pause]

Now listen again.

[repeat]

[pause]

This is the end of Part Two.
Now look at Part Three.

[pause]

PART 3   *Listen to Michael talking to Marina about a new sports centre.*
For questions 11–15, tick A, B or C.
You will hear the conversation twice.
Look at questions 11–15 now. You have 20 seconds.

[pause]

Now listen to the conversation.

Michael: Hello, Marina. Have you been to the new sports centre yet?
Marina: No, Michael, where is it?
Michael: In Long Road. You know, near Bridge Street, behind the station.
Marina: Oh. Is it good?
Michael: Yes, it's great! You can do a lot of sports. I played table-tennis and volleyball last week.
Marina: What about tennis?
Michael: Not yet. They're going to build some tennis courts next year.
Marina: Is it expensive?

95

Michael: Not really, Marina. It's £50 a year if you're 15 to 18, and £30 if you're under 15.

Marina: Oh, that's good because I'm still 14.

Michael: And on Tuesday, Thursday and Friday it stays open late – till 10 o'clock.

Marina: Oh, great. How did you get there?

Michael: I got the number 16 bus. It's only 10 minutes from the bus station. Do you want to go next week?

Marina: OK. Any day except Thursday.

Michael: Well, why don't we go on Friday? Then we can stay late.

Marina: Yes, OK. Let's meet after school.

[pause]

Now listen again.

[repeat]

[pause]

This is the end of Part Three.
Now look at Part Four.

[pause]

PART 4   *You will hear a conversation about a flat for rent.*
Listen and complete questions 16–20.
You will hear the conversation twice.

[pause]

Woman: Hello. Lonflats Agency. Can I help you?

Man: Oh yes. My name's Mark Jones. I'm phoning about the flat for rent in Putney. I saw the advertisement in the paper.

Woman: In Putney … Well, yes, Mr Jones, that one's got two bedrooms.

Man: Are they double bedrooms?

Woman: One double and one single.

Man: OK. And how much is the rent?

Woman: Well, it's £440 a month.

Man: I see. And where exactly is it?

Woman: It's number 27 Earsley Street.

Man: Oh. How do you spell that?

Woman: Earsley. It's E-A-R-S-L-E-Y. It's near the train station.

Man: And what floor is it on?

Woman: It's a second floor flat.

Man: Has it got any furniture?

Woman: Yes. It's got some nice modern furniture.

Man: Well. It sounds interesting. I'd like to see it, please.

Woman: Can you come tomorrow?

Man: Tomorrow. That's Tuesday?

Woman: Uh-hm.

Man: Well, only after 5 o'clock.

Woman: How about half past five?

Man: Yes, that's fine. Oh, one thing I nearly forgot. When will the flat be free to rent?

Woman: From the 1st of March.

Man: OK. See you tomorrow.

Woman: Bye.

[pause]

Now listen again.

[repeat]

[pause]

This is the end of Part Four.
Now look at Part Five.

[pause]

PART 5   *You will hear a tour guide talking about a day trip.*
Listen and complete questions 21–25.
You will hear the information twice.

[pause]

Guide: Hello everyone. I just want to tell you about our trip to the town of
        Chester. The coach will leave at nine fifteen tomorrow morning. It takes
        about an hour and a half to get to Chester, so we will arrive at a quarter
        to eleven. You will have time for a cup of coffee before our first visit. This
        will be to the castle. It is a very interesting old building and I'm sure you'll
        enjoy the visit. Tickets for the castle cost three pounds fifty for adults and,
        if you have children, a family ticket is just eight pounds. There are lots of
        things to see and we will be there about two hours.
        We will take sandwiches for lunch with us and we will all eat together in a
        park. You will be pleased to know that tomorrow is going to be sunny.
        After lunch, we will walk round the old market. You will be able to buy all
        your presents there. Now, any questions?

[pause]

Now listen again.

[repeat]

[pause]

This is the end of Part Five.

You now have eight minutes to write your answers on the answer sheet.

Note: Teacher, stop the recording here and time eight minutes. Remind students
when there is **one** minute remaining.

[pause]

This is the end of the test.

Test 3 Key

Paper 1   Reading and Writing

Part 1
1 E   2 C   3 A   4 G   5 B

Part 2
6 B   7 C   8 A   9 C   10 A

Part 3
11 A   12 B   13 C   14 B   15 C
16 B   17 F   18 H   19 A   20 E

Part 4
21 B   22 B   23 C   24 B   25 A   26 A   27 B

Part 5
28 A   29 B   30 A   31 C   32 B   33 B   34 A   35 C

Part 6
Spelling must be correct.
36 table   **37** cupboard   **38** shower   **39** window   **40** shelf

Part 7
For questions 41–50, ignore capitals/absence of capitals. Spelling must be correct.
41 to   **42** with   **43** at   **44** we   **45** this   **46** to/some
47 am/'m   **48** ask/invite/get   **49** you   **50** about

Part 8
For questions 51–55, spelling must be correct and capitals must be used where necessary.
51 23 Mount Road Oxford (England) (UK)   **52** Japanese
53 (computer) engineer   **54** (wife) Keiko (Ando)   **55** (Monday) 15(th) April

Part 9
Question 56
The note should include the following three pieces of information:
i   invitation
ii when and
iii where the party is.

98

Sample answer A

Mark: 5

There is only one minor spelling error (*posible*) and all three parts of the message are communicated clearly.

> *Hi Susi*
> *Would you like to come to the party with me today? The party is in my house at 7.00pm. If you are not busy today, please call me as soon as posible.*
> *See you!*
> *Alana*

Sample answer B

Mark: 4

All the points are mentioned but there are a number of errors in spelling and grammar.

> *Dear Khalid*
> *Next weekend I'am going with my family to have party in my saster's flat an south London, and I think you like it, an if you don;'t like coming can you tell me toumorw morning.*
> *Love Halim*

Sample answer C

Mark: 3

All three points are attempted but the invitation *I'd like to come* needs interpretation.

> *Dear Jack*
> *I have a party. Today my birth day. I'd like to come. The party will be at home at 10pm. See you there.*
> *Jasmin*

Sample answer D

Mark: 2

Two points of the message are communicated but there are a considerable number of errors that require patience and interpretation by the reader.

> *Dear Nasir*
> *Please come and guinte my Barthday party at 19.6.1998. Dear Nasir you mast gunite my Barlhday party in Friday evening at 10.0 klock.*
> *Thnk you*
> *Ali   If you cant guint the party pleese contakte my on 567891*

Sample answer E

Mark: 0

The candidate has not completed the task as required and cannot be given a mark.

> *Dear friend*
> *I am come to your party. What time your party start and when I come to your party and where have your party.*
> *See you soon*
> *Boris*

Paper 2   Listening

Part 1
1 A   **2** B   **3** C   **4** A   **5** C

Part 2
6 D   **7** C   **8** F   **9** A   **10** B

Part 3
11 B   **12** C   **13** A   **14** A   **15** B

Part 4
For questions 16–19, accept recognisable spelling. Spelling needs to be correct in question 20. Ignore capitals/absence of capitals.
16 (next) Monday   **17** (about) 15/fifteen (students)
18 12.99/twelve pounds ninety-nine   **19** nine/9 (o'clock)/9 a.m. to 1 p.m.
20 Green Park

Question 2   *Two*

How much petrol does the woman want?

Woman: Could you put 30 litres of petrol in my car, please?
Man: Did you say 13 litres?
Woman: No, 30 litres. Fill it up please.

[pause]

Now listen again.

[repeat]

[pause]

Question 3   *Three*

Which table do they buy?

Woman: Look – this round table is very nice.
Man: Yes, but it's made of plastic and it's only got three legs.
Woman: Do you want one with four legs?
Man: Yes – look, here's a square one. Let's have this.
Woman: OK.

[pause]

Now listen again.

[repeat]

[pause]

Question 4   *Four*

What time does the class start?

Boy: Are you going to the English class this afternoon, Susan?
Girl: Yes, it's at three o'clock, isn't it?
Boy: Two o'clock. I've got to go to the dentist's at half past two so I can't go.
Girl: Don't worry. I'll get the homework for you.

[pause]

Now listen again.

[repeat]

[pause]

Question 5   *Five*

What was the weather like on Emma's holiday?

Man: Did you enjoy your holiday in Australia, Emma?
Emma: Yes, but it was wet most of the time.
Man: Really? Isn't it always hot in Australia?
Emma: Mm. Not when I was there.

[pause]

Now listen again.

[repeat]

[pause]

Part 5

For questions 21–25, accept recognisable spelling. Ignore capitals/absence of capitals.

21 7/seven (hours)   **22** castle   **23** café/lunch   **24** beach/lake
25 camera

Transcript

This is the Key English Test. Paper 2. Listening. Test number three. There are five parts to the test. Parts One, Two, Three, Four and Five.

We will now stop for a moment before we start the test. Please ask any questions now because you mustn't speak during the test.

[pause]

PART 1   *Look at the instructions for Part One.*

[pause]

You will hear five short conversations.
You will hear each conversation twice.
There is one question for each conversation.
For questions 1–5, put a tick under the right answer.

Here is an example:
When's the school trip?

Boy: Are you going to go on the school trip, Maria?
Girl: Yes, I am.
Boy: It's on Wednesday, isn't it?
Girl: No, on Thursday. The bus leaves at 11 o'clock.

[pause]

The answer is Thursday, so there is a tick in box C.
Now we are ready to start.
Look at question one.

[pause]

Question 1   *One*
Where's the sports centre?

Man: Excuse me. Is the sports centre near here?
Woman: Yes, it's about ten minutes' walk. Go past the bank and take the second
             road on the left. It's on the corner.
Man: Thanks very much.

[pause]

Now listen again.

[repeat]

[pause]

This is the end of Part One.
Now look at Part Two.

[pause]

PART 2   *Listen to Jane talking to a friend about some clothes that she has bought for her*
holiday. What colours are her clothes?
For questions 6–10, write a letter, A–H, next to each of her clothes.
You will hear the conversation twice.

[pause]

Tim: Hi Jane. Have you been shopping?
Jane: Yes. I've bought some clothes. But I think I've got too many different
        colours.
Tim: Well, that's a nice white shirt. You can wear that with any colour.
Jane: Yes, I bought it in the same shop as this dress.
Tim: Let me see. Oh yes. What a lovely green! And have you bought a jacket to
        go with it?
Jane: Yes. It was difficult to find one but I finally got this dark brown one.
Tim: Oh yes – that's very nice. Did you buy anything else?
Jane: Well, I need a new sweater. I always wear this red one and it's so old now.
        So I bought this one.
Tim: Mmm – orange – that's an unusual colour.
Jane: Yes. I also bought a coat and some shoes.
Tim: You have been busy.
Jane: Yes. The coat was a bit expensive. Do you like it?
Tim: Oh yes. You look good in black. And those new black shoes look great with
        the coat.
Jane: Well, actually they're dark blue, not black.

[pause]

Now listen again.

[repeat]

[pause]

This is the end of Part Two.
Now look at Part Three.

[pause]

PART 3   *Listen to Mrs Lee talking to her secretary about her business trip.*
For questions 11–15, tick A, B or C.
You will hear the conversation twice.
Look at questions 11–15 now. You have 20 seconds.

[pause]

Now listen to the conversation.

Mrs Lee: So, tell me about my trip to Europe. Will I leave on Saturday or
              Sunday?
Secretary: I've booked your ticket for Saturday, Mrs Lee. Let me see, that's the
              11th and your plane leaves at 10 a.m.
Mrs Lee: So, I'll get to the airport at about eight.

Secretary: Yes. And you'll arrive in London at eleven fifty – you won't stop in Frankfurt this time. Mr Porter from our Amsterdam office will arrive at about the same time, so you can go together to your meeting at the factory – no time to go to the hotel, I'm afraid.

Mrs Lee: OK. And after the meeting?

Secretary: You'll have the afternoon free. Then in the evening you'll meet Jane and Peter Cook.

Mrs Lee: Is that at their home?

Secretary: Not this time. You're going to meet in a Japanese restaurant near your hotel. Then the next morning you'll go to Paris on the train.

Mrs Lee: Yes, that's better than flying again.

[pause]

Now listen again.

[repeat]

[pause]

This is the end of Part Three.
Now look at Part Four.

[pause]

PART 4   *Listen to a man asking for some information about a language school.*
Listen and complete questions 16–20.
You will hear the conversation twice.

[pause]

Woman: Hello, School of Italian Studies.

Man: Hello, I saw your advertisement in the newspaper. Can you give me some information, please?

Woman: Yes, of course. What would you like to know?

Man: Well, first, how long are the courses?

Woman: They're six or nine months long and the next courses begin next Monday.

Man: How many students will there be in the class? Not too many, I hope.

Woman: Usually, there are about 15. We find that a good number.

Man: OK. Now, I saw the price of the course in the newspaper, but will I have to pay for anything else?

Woman: Only for the coursebook, which costs twelve pounds ninety-nine.

Man: I see. When can I come and pay?

Woman: Well, the school is open eight a.m. to seven p.m. Monday to Friday and on Saturdays from nine to one.

Man: OK. And one more question – what's the nearest underground station to your school?

Woman: It's Green Park.

Man: Green Park. I see. Well, thank you very much. Goodbye.

Woman: Goodbye.

[pause]

Now listen again.

[repeat]

[pause]

This is the end of Part Four.
Now look at Part Five.

[pause]

PART 5   *You will hear a man talking about a day trip.*
Listen and complete questions 21–25.
You will hear the information twice.

[pause]

Tour guide: Hello everybody. Tomorrow we're all going on a coach trip to Lake
Tandy and I'd just like to give you some information about the trip.
   We'll be leaving here at nine thirty in the morning. It's a seven-
hour trip, so we'll be back at half past four. We're going to visit three
places. The first one is a castle. This was built six hundred years ago
and it is very interesting. After that we will stop at a café for lunch at
one o'clock. We'll stay there about three-quarters of an hour. We will
then drive on to our third stop. It will be at a beach and if you like you
can swim there or just sit in the sun and look at the scenery. The
lake is very beautiful and there are lots of birds there. So remember
to take a camera. I'm sure you'll be able to take some excellent
photographs.

[pause]

Now listen again.

[repeat]

[pause]

This is the end of Part Five.

You now have eight minutes to write your answers on the answer sheet.

Note: Teacher, stop the recording here and time eight minutes. Remind students
when there is **one** minute remaining.

[pause]

This is the end of the test.

Test 4 Key

Paper 1   Reading and Writing

Part 1
1 G   2 B   3 D   4 H   5 A

Part 2
6 A   7 A   8 B   9 C   10 C

Part 3
11 C   12 A   13 A   14 A   15 B
16 E   17 F   18 B   19 H   20 G

Part 4
21 B   22 B   23 A   24 C   25 A   26 B   27 A

Part 5
28 B   29 A   30 B   31 A   32 A   33 A   34 B   35 C

Part 6
Spelling must be correct.
36 shoes   37 suit   38 raincoat   39 shorts   40 sweater

Part 7
For questions 41–50, ignore capitals/absence of capitals. Spelling must be correct.
41 told   42 had/decided/have   43 are   44 a   45 the   46 were
47 me   48 you   49 to   50 on/next

Part 8
For questions 51–55, spelling must be correct and capitals must be used where necessary.
51 21(st) May   52 Paris   53 18.25/6.25 p.m.   54 one/a/1/suitcase
55 clothes

Part 9
Question 56
The note should include the following three pieces of information:

i   request to return cassette recorder
ii why you need it and
iii when you need it.

Sample answer A

Mark: 5

The three points are covered clearly and fully with only occasional grammatical errors.

> *Dear Chris*
> *Hello Chris, do you remember that I lent you my cassette*
> *recorder? Yes, I'm very sure that you can remember. But I need to*
> *use that cassette recorder. I'll use it to help me in the class*
> *because my teachers speak very fast. I'll need it on Friday. So you*
> *must bring it to me on Thursday*
> *Thank you*
> *Korin*

Sample answer B

Mark: 4

All three parts of the message are communicated with some errors in spelling and grammar.

> *Dear Chris*
> *It's well my cassette recorder? I need the cassette recorder*
> *because I have to record a cassette to Mary. i need the cassette*
> *the next week.*
> *Best whishes*
> *Rosa*

Sample answer C

Mark: 3

All three parts of the message have been attempted but *in the all in the morning* requires interpretation. There are also grammatical errors.

> *Dear Chris*
> *You have my cassette recorder, I must leave the cassette at my*
> *friend for holiday, you leave the cassette in the all in the morning,*
> *because in the afternoon, I leave the city.*
> *Thank you*
> *Mira*

Sample answer D

Mark: 3

The language is clear and accurate and would score a 5 if all three points had been included. However, the reason has been omitted.

> *Chris: Hallo, I need my cassette recorder. Could you come to my house to give it to me because I need it for today. Thank you.*

Sample answer E

Mark: 1

Only one point is communicated; the final sentence is copied from the rubric.

> *Hi Chris, yesterday I gave you my cassette recorder. I'd like that my cassette recorder return to me. And why and when you need it?*

Paper 2   Listening

Part 1
1 B   **2** A   **3** C   **4** C   **5** A

Part 2
6 B   **7** D   **8** A   **9** G   **10** H

Part 3
11 A   **12** B   **13** B   **14** A   **15** C

Part 4

For questions 16–20, ignore capitals/absence of capitals. In questions 16 and 19 spelling must be correct.

16 Friday   **17** 8.30/half past eight/eight thirty   **18** London Hotel
19 SHINDY (Street)   **20** pencil(s)

Part 5

For questions 21–24, accept recognisable spelling. Ignore capitals/absence of capitals. In question 25 spelling must be correct.

21 Midnight (Meeting)   **22** Thursday
23 (6.45 and) 9.15(p.m.) quarter past nine   **24** 2.80   **25** HAUXTON

Transcript

This is the Key English Test. Paper 2. Listening. Test number four. There are five parts to the test. Parts One, Two, Three, Four and Five.

We will now stop for a moment before we start the test. Please ask any questions now because you mustn't speak during the test.

[pause]

PART 1   *Look at the instructions for Part One.*

[pause]

You will hear five short conversations.
You will hear each conversation twice.
There is one question for each conversation.
For questions 1–5, put a tick under the right answer.

Here is an example:
What time is it?

Woman: Excuse me, can you tell me the time?
Man: Yes, it's 9 o'clock.
Woman: Thank you.
Man: You're welcome.

[pause]

The answer is nine o'clock, so there is a tick in box C.
Now we are ready to start.
Look at question one.

[pause]

Question 1   *One*

What was the weather like on Wednesday?

Woman: What was the weather like when you were on holiday?
Man: Fine; it was sunny every day until Wednesday.
Woman: Really? What happened then?
Man: Well, it was sunny in the morning, but it rained in the afternoon.

[pause]

Now listen again.

[repeat]

[pause]

Question 2   *Two*

How much did Mark's pullover cost?

Woman: That's a nice pullover, Mark – was it expensive?
Mark: Mmm. Fourteen pounds ninety-nine.
Woman: Oh, that's not bad.
Mark: No, and I do like blue.

[pause]

Now listen again.

[repeat]

[pause]

Question 3 *Three*

What did Raquel buy today?

Tina: Hi, Raquel. You're looking well. New skirt?

Raquel: Thanks Tina. No, I've had this skirt for a long time. I bought these boots this morning. Do you like them?

Tina: Yes, very nice. They look good with that jacket.

[pause]

Now listen again.

[repeat]

[pause]

Question 4 *Four*

How many students are there at the college?

Girl: How many students are there at your college?

Boy: Oh, there's lots. It's quite a big college.

Girl: More than three hundred?

Boy: Oh yes, more than twice that. About seven hundred and fifty, I think.

[pause]

Now listen again.

[repeat]

[pause]

Question 5 *Five*

What is David going to buy?

Woman: Hi, David. What are you looking for?

David: I don't know what to buy for Rachel's birthday.

Woman: Well, I've bought her a CD, so why don't you get her a book?

David: Yes, that's a good idea – I will.

[pause]

Now listen again.

[repeat]

[pause]

This is the end of Part One.
Now look at Part Two.

[pause]

PART 2 *Listen to Philip talking to his mother about his son, Simon.*
What is Simon going to do on Saturday and Sunday?
For questions 6–10, write a letter, A–H, next to each time of day.
You will hear the conversation twice.

[pause]

Philip: Well, Mum, thanks for having Simon to stay for a couple of days.

Mother: That's OK, Philip. What have I got to do?

Philip: Well, Saturday's busy. In the morning he's got his judo class.

Mother: Right, and in the afternoon he's going to a birthday party, isn't he?

Philip: No, that's in the evening. He's going to the football match in the afternoon, remember?

Mother: Oh yes, I remember now. So what time does the party start?

Philip: At half past seven, but Mrs Carter'll bring him home.

Mother: Fine. Now on Sunday morning, we can go to the swimming pool on our bikes.

Philip: Well, … he's got a cold, so swimming isn't a very good idea, but he'd like a bicycle ride.

Mother: OK. Your father wants to take Simon to the park in the afternoon.

Philip: Fine. And then a quiet evening watching TV.

Mother: What about a trip to the cinema?

Philip: No. I think he'll be too tired for that.

Mother: OK.

[pause]

Now listen again.

[repeat]

[pause]

This is the end of Part Two.
Now look at Part Three.

[pause]

PART 3   *Listen to Chloe talking to a man about a sailing holiday.*
For questions 11–15, tick A, B or C.
You will hear the conversation twice.
Look at questions 11–15 now. You have 20 seconds.

[pause]

Now listen to the conversation.

Man: Hello, can I help you?

Chloe: Yes, I'd like to go on a sailing holiday this summer in Italy.

Man: Have you been sailing before?

Chloe: No. I wanted to go to Sweden last year, but I didn't have enough money.

Man: Well, it is quite expensive. Sailing holidays start at about three hundred pounds.

Chloe: Yes, my friends went in August last year. They paid four hundred and fifty pounds each. The most I can pay is three hundred and eighty pounds.

Man: Well, that should be enough.

Chloe: When's the cheapest time to go?

Man: Well, August is the most expensive month. September and October are cheaper.

Chloe: October's too late for me, so I'll go in September.

Man: Would you like to be by the sea or a lake?

Chloe: Well, I'd prefer a lake in the mountains.

Man: OK. The Aqua Centre in north Italy will be best for you. That costs £370.

Chloe: OK. Can I pay by credit card? I haven't got my cheque book.

Man: Yes, that's fine.

[pause]

Now listen again.

[repeat]

[pause]

This is the end of Part Three.
Now look at Part Four.

[pause]

PART 4   *You will hear Kate and Jeremy talking about a party.*
    Listen and complete questions 16–20.
    You will hear the conversation twice.

[pause]

Jeremy: Hello.

Kate: Hi Jeremy. It's Kate. I'm going to have a party next week. Would you like to come to it?

Jeremy: A party – that's great. What's it for?

Kate: It's my birthday on Wednesday – I'm going to be seventeen.

Jeremy: Oh dear – I can't come on Wednesday.

Kate: No – my birthday's Wednesday, but the party's on Friday.

Jeremy: Oh, that's OK. What time will it begin?

Kate: At eight thirty.

Jeremy: Right – that should be no problem.

Kate: It's going to be at the London Hotel. Do you know where that is?

Jeremy: Let me think – the London Hotel. No, I don't.

Kate: Well, it's near the town centre on Shindy Street.

Jeremy: Could you spell that for me?

Kate: Yeah, sure. It's S-H-I-N-D-Y – Shindy Street.

Jeremy: OK. I can find that. I've got a map. Can I bring anything?

Kate: Well, I need a lot of pencils for a game we're going to play.

Jeremy: OK. I'll bring some pencils.

Kate: Thanks. See you there.

[pause]

Now listen again.

[repeat]

[pause]

This is the end of Part Four.
Now look at Part Five.

[pause]

PART 5   *You will hear some information about a cinema.*
Listen and complete questions 21–25.
You will hear the information twice.

[pause]

Woman: Thank you for calling the North London Arts Cinema, Wood Green.
There is no one to answer your call at the moment.

The North London Arts Cinema is open seven days a week, showing
a variety of British and foreign films.

Next week we will show an Italian film called *Midnight Meeting*. It is
set in Milan in the 1950s. You can see that film from Monday to
Thursday. It will be on twice a day in the evenings. That's at 6.45 and
9.15. The film lasts two hours and fifteen minutes. Tickets are £4, but
there is a special student ticket at £2.80 for all our midweek films.
Please bring your student card if you want the cheaper ticket.

The nearest car park to the cinema is in Hauxton Street. That's
H-A-U-X-T-O-N. It's just five minutes' walk from the cinema.

Thank you for calling the North London Arts Cinema. If you require
further information, phone during office hours – 9 a.m. to 4.30 p.m.,
Monday to Friday.

[pause]

Now listen again.

[repeat]

[pause]

This is the end of Part Five.

You now have eight minutes to write your answers on the answer sheet.

Note: Teacher, stop the recording here and time eight minutes. Remind the
students when there is **one** minute remaining.

[pause]

This is the end of the test.

Sample answer sheet – Reading and Writing (Sheet 1)

UNIVERSITY *of* **CAMBRIDGE**
ESOL Examinations

S A M P L E

Candidate Name
If not already printed, write name
in CAPITALS and complete the
Candidate No. grid (in pencil).

Candidate Signature

Examination Title

Centre

Supervisor:
If the candidate is ABSENT or has WITHDRAWN shade here ▭

Centre No.

Candidate No.

Examination
Details

0	0	0	0
1	1	1	1
2	2	2	2
3	3	3	3
4	4	4	4
5	5	5	5
6	6	6	6
7	7	7	7
8	8	8	8
9	9	9	9

KET Paper 1 Reading and Writing Candidate Answer Sheet

Instructions

Use a PENCIL (B or HB).
Rub out any answer you want to change with an eraser.

For **Parts 1, 2, 3, 4** and **5:**
Mark ONE letter for each question.
For example, if you think **C** is the right answer to the
question, mark your answer sheet like this:

| 0 | A B C |

Part 1

1	A B C D E F G H
2	A B C D E F G H
3	A B C D E F G H
4	A B C D E F G H
5	A B C D E F G H

Part 2

6	A B C
7	A B C
8	A B C
9	A B C
10	A B C

Part 3

11	A B C
12	A B C
13	A B C
14	A B C
15	A B C

16	A B C D E F G H
17	A B C D E F G H
18	A B C D E F G H
19	A B C D E F G H
20	A B C D E F G H

Part 4

21	A B C
22	A B C
23	A B C
24	A B C
25	A B C
26	A B C
27	A B C

Part 5

28	A B C
29	A B C
30	A B C
31	A B C
32	A B C
33	A B C
34	A B C
35	A B C

**Turn over for
Parts 6 - 9** →

© UCLES K&J **Photocopiable**

Sample answer sheet – Reading and Writing (Sheet 2)

For **Parts 6, 7 and 8:**

Write your answers in the spaces next to the numbers (36 to 55) like this:

0	example

Part 6		Do not write here
36		1 36 0
37		1 37 0
38		1 38 0
39		1 39 0
40		1 40 0

Part 7		Do not write here
41		1 41 0
42		1 42 0
43		1 43 0
44		1 44 0
45		1 45 0
46		1 46 0
47		1 47 0
48		1 48 0
49		1 49 0
50		1 50 0

Part 8		Do not write here
51		1 51 0
52		1 52 0
53		1 53 0
54		1 54 0
55		1 55 0

Part 9 (Question 56): Write your answer below.

Do not write below (Examiner use only)					
0	1	2	3	4	5

Sample answer sheet – Listening

UNIVERSITY *of* CAMBRIDGE
ESOL Examinations

S A M P L E

Candidate Name
If not already printed, write name
in CAPITALS and complete the
Candidate No. grid (in pencil).

Candidate Signature

Examination Title

Centre

Centre No.

Candidate No.

Examination
Details

0	0	0	0
1	1	1	1
2	2	2	2
3	3	3	3
4	4	4	4
5	5	5	5
6	6	6	6
7	7	7	7
8	8	8	8
9	9	9	9

Supervisor:
If the candidate is ABSENT or has WITHDRAWN shade here

KET Paper 2 Listening Candidate Answer Sheet

Instructions

Use a PENCIL (B or HB).

Rub out any answer you want to change with an eraser.

For **Parts 1, 2** and **3**:
Mark ONE letter for each question.
For example, if you think **C** is the right answer to the
question, mark your answer sheet like this:

0   A   B   C

Part 1

1	A B C
2	A B C
3	A B C
4	A B C
5	A B C

Part 2

6	A B C D E F G H
7	A B C D E F G H
8	A B C D E F G H
9	A B C D E F G H
10	A B C D E F G H

Part 3

11	A B C
12	A B C
13	A B C
14	A B C
15	A B C

For **Parts 4** and **5**:
Write your answers in the spaces next to the
numbers (16 to 25) like this:

0   *example*

Part 4		Do not write here
16		1 16 0
17		1 17 0
18		1 18 0
19		1 19 0
20		1 20 0

Part 5		Do not write here
21		1 21 0
22		1 22 0
23		1 23 0
24		1 24 0
25		1 25 0